Stay the Course

# Endorsements for
## *Stay the Course*

As a practicing family physician for over 35 years, I've counseled many high school graduates as they prepared to leave home for college. This is a stress-filled time for both the student and their parents. I'm so thankful for Dr. Katherine Pasour's new devotional, *Stay the Course*, dedicated to helping them navigate this new territory. Tying each devotion to scripture and using her own personal stories from years as a college professor, anchor her words with wisdom. It's a sad fact that the drop-out rate for incoming freshman after the first semester remains high. I'm already thinking of the young people I know going into their senior year of high school who would benefit from this wonderful reference full of solid advice to help them stay the course.

**–Suzanne Montgomery MD,** staff physician,
Ascension Health Employer
Dedicated Wellness Centers

Dr. Katherine Pasour offers practical tips and considerations for college students through relevant application of Biblical principles. Katherine highlights key topics for students that can lead to a successful transition to new and exciting experiences while staying focused on God for guidance and strength. *Stay the Course* is a must for all college students.

**–Dr. Dawn Day,** Chair and Professor of Graduate Nursing Programs–Spring Arbor University, Spring Arbor, Michigan

Dr. Katherine Pasour has crafted a unique addition to first year experience reading options with *Stay the Course: A Devotional Handbook to Survive and Thrive in Your First Year of College (and Beyond)*. Her long experience in working with first-year students is clearly evident in this collection of very real dilemmas every first year student faces. Her positive, yet direct, offering of each issue will speak to students in a way college students will find honest and respectful. The brevity Pasour has chosen aligns with the young adult developing brain and will keep students engaged. Including appropriate scripture throughout the text opens doors for use not only in first year experience courses, but also with audiences in youth groups planning college transition programs that could substantively engage families to better understand and support their student's first year journey. *Stay the*

*Course: A Devotional Handbook to Survive and Thrive in Your First Year of College (and Beyond)* is a welcome addition to the first year reading collection!

**–Dr. Gail Summer,** Former Vice President of Academic Affairs, Ferrum College, Virginia, Retired

DR. KATHERINE PASOUR

# Stay
## —the—
# Course

*A Devotional Handbook
to* SURVIVE *and* THRIVE
*in Your First Year of
College* (AND BEYOND)

NASHVILLE

NEW YORK • LONDON • MELBOURNE • VANCOUVER

# Stay the Course

## A Devotional Handbook to Survive and Thrive in Your First Year of College (and Beyond)

Published in New York, New York, by Morgan James Publishing. Morgan James is a trademark of Morgan James, LLC. www.MorganJamesPublishing.com

Proudly distributed by Publishers Group West®

Scripture taken from THE HOLY BIBLE, NEW INTERNATIONAL VERSION®. Copyright© 1973, 1978, 1984, 2011 by Biblica, Inc.™. Used by permission of Zondervan.

Student names and identifying details have been changed to protect the privacy of individuals.

A **FREE** ebook edition is available for you
or a friend with the purchase of this print book.

CLEARLY SIGN YOUR NAME ABOVE

**Instructions to claim your free ebook edition:**
1. Visit MorganJamesBOGO.com
2. Sign your name CLEARLY in the space above
3. Complete the form and submit a photo of this entire page
4. You or your friend can download the ebook to your preferred device

ISBN 9781636982724 paperback
ISBN 9781636982731 ebook
Library of Congress Control Number:
2023942600

**Cover & Interior Design by:**
Christopher Kirk
www.GFSstudio.com

Morgan James is a proud partner of Habitat for Humanity Peninsula and Greater Williamsburg. Partners in building since 2006.

Get involved today! Visit: www.morgan-james-publishing.com/giving-back

# Table of Contents

# Introduction

If you are reading this devotional, you're most likely a new high school graduate (or a parent or guardian of a recent graduate). This is a new, exciting, and marvelous adventure for the new graduate and your family. The decision to attend college is a serious commitment, one that you and your parents have considered for many years.

Now the time has come. The next four (or more years) will determine your future path. The higher education experience can be some of the most joyful years of your life. College may also be the most challenging and terrifying experience you have yet faced. Whether you realize it, you will need advice, encouragement, and support on this new journey. You are crossing the bridge onto a new road, from childhood and adolescence into adulthood. There will be mountains to climb, rough and rocky trails to hike, and valleys to overcome. You will experience periods of elation, happiness, and success, as well as times of fear, despair, and depression.

These devotions are a practical and spiritual guide for your summer of preparation and your first year of

college. With God as your guide, you will meet challenges with confidence to *survive and thrive* in your first
year of college and beyond.

The individual devotions are short—the life of a college student is a busy one, so a quick read is ideal for
you. Devotions are grouped by themes and introduced
with a story related to the focus of that category. Each
individual segment within the theme includes Scripture
relevant to the topic, a brief story or example, practical
advice to assist you on your journey, and prayer.

This devotional begins with recommendations to
assist you in the summer following high school graduation to "get ready" for the new challenges of college.
Establishing a good beginning during the first week of
classes is your jump-start to a victorious first semester
and continued success on the road to completing your
degree. The Table of Contents displays the categories
of focus when situations arise that require extra wisdom
and insight to be resolved. While the beginning of the
book has a specific focus on summer preparation and
a successful first week, additional sections can be read
consecutively through the semester or out of order as
needed for assistance in a particular area.

In my twenty-five years of working with college students, I mentored many young men and women through
the challenge of their first year of college. Much of the
advice and guidelines you read in this book are strate-

gies used successfully to assist students in adapting to the many challenges of being a first-year student while developing habits to foster a successful and rewarding college experience and preparing for life beyond.

Always remember—family, friends, your college faculty, and your fellow students want college to be an enjoyable and worthwhile experience for you. And, most importantly, our Lord wants to be with you on this journey.

> You make known to me the path of life; you will fill me with joy in your presence, with eternal pleasures at your right hand.
>
> **Psalm 16:11**

As the psalmist wrote, there will be joy and pleasure, and God will make your path known. You will find God on the mountaintop of happiness and hope, and He will be with you in the valley of worry and apprehension. God will be with you on your new journey.

*May God's grace and love shine on you!*

*Katherine Pasour*

# Getting Ready to Stay the Course

Summer is a time to prepare for your new journey.

## PREPARATION CAN DETERMINE RESULTS

Peaches and I went through fire together.

Muscles quivered and contracted in preparation to flee as smoke filled the crowded arena. A ribbon of flame raced across the ground as the jostling crowd milled about in confusion, squealing in fear. Sirens, shouting, and gunshots added fuel to the flame of terror that coursed through the veins of person and beast. A terrified snort preceded an attempted escape toward the side gate.

Peaches is my horse, and I, just as terrified, was riding. Horses are, by nature, fearful of the unknown. As prey animals, their first instinct is to run from danger, to escape a predator or any circumstance that causes fear.

We had signed up for a De-Spook Clinic. Or rather, I did. Peaches was a most reluctant participant. A frightening series of stations consisted of strips of tarps snapping in the wind; scary obstacles to go over, under, and through; wailing sirens; a shouting man with a gun, whistle, and megaphone and . . . a dog—a big, barking, aggressive dog that nipped at already terrified equines.

Peaches immediately went into flight mode to bolt from danger and the chaotic mass of terrified horses and struggling riders. "Get away. Run!" She signaled me with ragged breathing, wide eyes, tossing head, and dancing hooves.

My tension was nearly as great as hers. *Why am I doing this?*

God came to Moses in Midian, appearing in the burning bush that was not consumed. Moses was frightened but curious—and he went closer. God commanded Moses to go to Egypt to rescue the Israelites and bring them to the land of "milk and honey." But Moses was scared (who wouldn't be?) and hesitant to take on this terrifying responsibility.

> But Moses said to God, "Who am I that I should go to Pharaoh and bring the Israelites out of Egypt?"
>
> **Exodus 3:11**

Moses had all sorts of excuses. He feared Pharaoh would not respect him or listen when confronted with demands to release the Israelites. Moses complained about his lack of eloquence in speaking. In response, God demonstrated His awesome power and spoke of the actions He would bring against the Egyptians. He provided Aaron to speak for Moses (Exodus 3:19–4:17). Although still fearful, Moses stepped out in faith and obeyed. With God's guidance through the many challenges required to force Pharaoh to release the Israelites and the journey that followed, God kept His promises. Moses submitted to his Lord's commands, and God was steadfast and trustworthy in response.

Peaches and I spent two long and horrifying days at this clinic. She was reluctant. I was persistent. We became partners, working together to survive all sorts of torture the retired police officer put us through to accustom horse and rider to anything and everything that might frighten a horse.

There was plenty to terrify *both* horse and rider.

So why did we do this? Besides the concept of getting the horse accustomed to scary situations, the other main goals of the weekend were to build trust between horse and rider and facilitate complete submission of the horse to the rider. The horse submits and trusts the rider to be in charge, to set the pathway and direction of action. The two become a cohesive team, and they can accomplish great things together.

Submission and trust . . .

We've perhaps heard those terms somewhere else.

> Trust in the Lord with all your heart and lean not upon your own understanding; in all your ways, submit to him and he will make your paths straight.
>
> **Proverbs 3:5–6**

Between horse and rider, submission of the horse to the rider is essential. Otherwise, the relationship is a failure. If the horse won't obey the rider, nothing can be accomplished. In fact, failure to obey the rider can place both horse and rider in danger. But, when trust is developed between the two, great things result.

The horse doesn't always give up control easily. We begin training horses from birth to prepare them for their future role. We touch and handle the foal frequently to get them accustomed to human contact. At a young age, the horse is taught to follow its master when led by a halter, to respond to changes of direction when commanded, and to behave with respect and obedience toward its trainer. Learning obedience doesn't occur overnight—it requires ongoing effort, a commitment to **stay the course.** Training a horse is a long-term process with much repetition, practice, encouragement, and discipline.

Several years of training occurred before Peaches and I completed this clinic designed to help horses and riders work through their fears. We had the foundation of many hours of cooperative work to build upon before being initiated into this frightful weekend. If we hadn't already practiced submission and built up a basic level of trust, we would have failed in the de-spooking experience. Some horses are so fearful and untrusting that they run away when faced with terrors they don't understand. Sometimes the rider gets tossed in the process, and the horse and rider must go back to the basics of establishing obedience and rebuilding trust.

The progression is much the same when we humans are developing our relationship with our Lord. Often we struggle with giving up control. Many times a pastor, teacher, or mentor helps us through the painful process of achieving obedience to God. As with training a horse, daily practice, repetition, much patience, and self-discipline are required as we nurture our relationship with our Father.

And when we rebel against the training? It can be a disaster for horses and riders, but also for us. When Jonah was called by God to go to Nineveh, he fled from God's command, refusing to trust his Lord's directive to preach repentance to the wicked people of the city (Jonah 1). Jonah's disobedience and God's reaction threatened the lives of sailors and passengers on the ship Jonah chose for his escape.

But when we trust and submit to our Lord, we are given safety and security through the power of His love.

Peaches and I were terrified for much of our weekend of de-spook training. Yet, we gained trust in each other;

we stayed the course as we conquered the obstacles set before us and emerged victorious. Facing our fears of submission and trust in giving over complete control to God are much the same. It is a conscious decision we make—trust and submit. Initially, as we accept Jesus as our Savior, we acknowledge our trust in our Lord. Submission may be a greater challenge, and one that we must re-commit to daily. But the reward we receive is beyond measure. Our Lord will delight in us, and we will bear fruit.

> But blessed is the one who trusts in the Lord, whose confidence is in him. They will be like a tree planted by the water that sends out roots to the stream. It does not fear when heat comes; its leaves are always green. It has no worries in a year of drought and never fails to bear fruit.
>
> **Jeremiah 17:7–8**

Your college experience has many similarities to the challenges Peaches and I felt during this clinic. You will face new and difficult experiences, problems you may not initially know how to solve, and trials that tempt you to run away. Advance preparation will help, but you will also learn a great deal along the way of your journey.

**Stay the course!** You already have a strong foundation from your years of schooling and encouragement from your family and support group. Even though you will face challenges and trials on this new journey of college, there will be help along the way. You will have mentors and build trusting relationships with others. As God was with Moses and equipped him to successfully meet his challenges, God will also be with you.

# ESTABLISH PLANS

Commit to the Lord whatever you do, and he will establish your plans.

**Proverbs 16:3**

You've completed a major milestone—high school graduation.

CONGRATULATIONS!

Now is the time to prepare for the next part of your journey: college. Now, that's a scary thought! You're likely excited and apprehensive at the same time. You can take actions during the summer to help pave the way toward success as a college student.

By this time, you've likely decided on your college or university. Hopefully, you've already visited, perhaps even more than once. If convenient and financially possible, another visit to campus during the summer is a good idea. Take time to familiarize yourself with the campus. Know where the classroom buildings, library, financial aid, student affairs, student support services, and cafeteria are located. If you're living on campus, visit your residence hall, if possible. Ask questions.

Have you had student orientation yet? Take time to listen carefully to your guide. It's hard to remember all the helpful advice but do your best to be attentive during all aspects of orientation. **Ask questions**. Even if you've attended orientation and had a campus tour, it's still a good idea to visit again. Each new visit will provide additional insight and assist you in adapting to your new environment when you move.

***Did I remind you to ask questions?*** You won't realize how much you don't know until school begins.

> *Prayer: Father, I'm a high school graduate! This new road is kind of scary. Sometimes the thought of going to college is terrifying. I pray you will guide me and all new students to be prepared and help us know what questions to ask.*

# GETTING READY TO KNOW AND GROW

So that you may live a life worthy of the Lord and please him in every way; bearing fruit in every good work, growing in the knowledge of God, being strengthened with all power according to his glorious might so that you may have great endurance and patience.

**Colossians 1:10–11**

Graduation from high school is a major milestone in your life—one more step on the road to adulthood. You've needed endurance, perseverance, and patience to achieve this goal.

Great job!

Those same traits will serve you well as you continue your education. College is like merging onto an interstate highway. It's an accelerated and more complicated path toward your future. Navigating on this road requires necessary equipment (more than just a car).

For your journey, you will need:

- Adequate preparation (your academic foundation).
- A good map (plan) to reach your destination.
- Careful observation of obstacles, roadblocks, and pitfalls and discernment to avoid hazards or make a change of direction when needed.

- Perseverance, hard work, and support to keep you on the road (and not lost).
- An attitude of self-reflection.
- Adequate fuel (good nutrition and healthy habits).
- To keep your eyes, mind, and effort on the destination.

Whether you live at home and commute or move away for college, it's a huge adjustment. The better prepared you are for academic rigor and challenge, the more likely you are to achieve your goal of completing your degree.

Part of your preparation should be some self-analysis. What areas might you need to work on this summer?

*Prayer: Many of us are getting ready for college. Like me, most students are probably confident and terrified at the same time. We probably don't know what we don't know. Please help us understand what we need to do to help prepare us for this new journey.*

## Prepare Ahead

---

Jesus sent Peter and John, saying, "Go and make preparations for us to eat the Passover."

"Where do you want us to prepare for it?" they asked.

**Luke 22:8–9**

Jesus provided specific directions to his disciples about how to prepare for the Passover (Luke 22:10–12). Jesus presented an organized plan, and the disciples prepared accordingly.

Your plan for the summer can include actions to prepare for college:

- Consider taking a summer class to get an early start. That could lighten your load for the first semester.
- If you take a course elsewhere (such as your local community college), get approval in advance from the institution you plan to attend in the fall.
- Plan a visit to your campus.
- If you intend to work on campus during the fall semester, check your job location and plan a meeting with your supervisor.
- Check if your instructors have chosen or posted textbooks for their class. If so, shop for the best prices and get your books early.

- Some texts may be online. Investigate when those are available for purchase and download.
- Familiarize yourself (skim through) your textbooks before the semester begins. Prepare any questions you wish to ask your instructor.
- Some institutions assign a book reading or some other task to first-year students. If this is the case for you, remember to complete the assignment and do it well.
- If you are living on campus and plan to have a roommate, ask for their name, address, and contact information. Meeting your roommate in advance can ease the adjustment when the semester begins.

*Prayer: Father, I know advance planning can help me better prepare for college. Please guide me through this summer of preparation.*

# CHECK OUT THE SERVICES OFFERED AT YOUR SCHOOL

*Ask and it will be given to you, seek and you will find, knock and the door will be open for you.*

**Matthew 7:7**

Summer is an excellent time to investigate the services offered by your chosen college or university. The campus website is a good place to begin. Although you may not yet realize the differing demands of college academics or recognize the type of help you might need, the more you familiarize yourself with the services offered, the easier it will be once you are on campus.

The names will vary from campus to campus, but the services will be similar. Your campus may offer:

- Academic coaching.
- Tutoring (both one-on-one and group tutoring in a variety of areas).
- Assistance to improve writing skills.
- Assistance to improve study skills.
- Learning labs in a specific discipline (math, computer science, public speaking, etc.).
- A health center and counseling assistance.
- Accessibility services.

- Internship and volunteer opportunities.
- Wellness programs.

Your campus may extend even more opportunities for assistance. Read what your website has to say about each of the services. When you arrive at school, tour the campus and locate the office for each.

Recognizing when you need help and seeking assistance is a sign of strength and ownership of the issue. Asking for help is a proactive strategy to keep you on course for a successful first year, and the years that follow, culminating in graduation.

*Prayer: Father, as I prepare for the big step of going to college, help me be confident but not too stubborn to seek help if I need it. I pray you will guide me to recognize when I need to seek advice and assistance from on-campus services.*

## Learn about a Budget

Suppose one of you wants to build a tower. Won't you first sit down and estimate the cost to see if you have enough money to complete it?

**Luke 14:28**

You already know that a college education isn't free or cheap. Whether you're attending on scholarship or loans or someone is footing your bill, tuition must be paid. No matter where the money comes from, chances are your family is paying a significant amount. With scholarships or loans, conditions may be attached as to how and when the money is to be used. If a loan, you are obligated to pay the money back after you graduate or leave school.

If you haven't already learned how to create a budget, this summer is a good time to develop one. It's not just your tuition that requires payment. Consider room and board (if you're not commuting), textbooks, additional fees associated with particular classes, fuel costs, eating out, and personal expenses. If you're renting or leasing an apartment, you have rent, utility costs, groceries, and other expenses related to maintaining your household.

If you've maintained a job to pay some of your personal expenses, you've already gained some experience with budgeting. You have a good foundation for facing the additional responsibilities of developing your educational budget. It's still a good idea to consult with your parents or guardians to learn more about managing your finances. Careful oversight of spending can help your funds last longer and reduce your long-term burden of student loans. Online Financial Literacy Programs are available and can be a useful aspect of your summer preparation plan.

> *Prayer: Father, another part of my new journey is being responsible for my expenses at school. Please help me be wise in my expenditures and help me be responsible in establishing and sticking to a reasonable budget.*

# FAMILY

Honor your father and your mother, so that you may live long in the land the Lord your God is giving you.

**Exodus 20:12**

Not all of us have what is typically called a "traditional family." Many come from blended families, single-parent families, or households with extended family. You may have a guardian or live with someone not biologically related to you. But, no matter the structure of your family, there are people who love and care for you. These are the folks to whom I'm referring.

As you prepare to leave home—or even attend college in your hometown—keep in mind that you are embarking on a new aspect of your life. Things will never be quite the same again. Take time this summer to be with family. Plan activities where you all can enjoy time together.

This new period in your life involves a change for your parents, guardians, or extended family. They are recognizing that the child has become an adult. This period of adjustment will affect your family. While they are very proud of the young adult you have become, they miss the child. Make a special effort to share love with them before you begin school in the fall. A letter to your parents or family expressing your appreciation for their care and guidance is a gift from you they will forever cherish.

> *Prayer: Father, I know I will miss my family, even though I've been looking forward to college. There will be times when I will need their guidance. Help me know when to ask them for advice. I pray that I adjust quickly and get off to a good start. Please take care of my family and keep them safe.*

# Faith, Hope, and Love

And now these three remain: faith, hope, and love. But the greatest of these is love.

**1 Corinthians 13:13**

As you mentally prepare for this upcoming college journey, keep in mind faith, hope, and love.

Now faith is confidence in what we hope for and assurance about what we do not see.

**Hebrews 11:1**

Your family has faith and confidence in you. You will succeed in your goals to get off to a good start in college, work hard to be successful, and achieve your plan to graduate. You can be assured that God also wants you to achieve your goals.

"For I know the plans I have for you," declares the Lord, "plans to prosper you and not to harm you, plans to give you a hope and a future."

**Jeremiah 29:11**

God has a plan for you. Remember to hold on to the love.

Love is patient, love is kind. It does not envy, it does not boast, it is not proud. It does not dishonor others, it is not self-seeking, it is not easily angered, it keeps no record of wrongs. Love does not delight in evil but rejoices in the truth. It always protects, always trusts, always hopes, always perseveres.

**1 Corinthians 13:4–7**

Keep **faith** in yourself. Hold on to the **hope** of God's plan for your future. **Love** your family, your neighbors (students and faculty), and yourself (take care of yourself).

Faith, hope, and love will guide you through this time of preparation and keep you safely on the path to college graduation.

*Prayer: God, I know you have a plan for me. Your Word tells me that. Help me stay on your path to graduation. Please guide me to love others at home and school.*

# YOUR PLANS ARE NOBLE

But, the noble make noble plans, and by noble deeds they stand.

**Isaiah 32:8**

You've graduated high school; you plan to complete college and prepare for a career.

Your plans are noble. Noble deeds will be accomplished.

But your plan will need diligent and consistent effort to reach fulfillment. You'll need a combination of perseverance, flexibility, and determination to succeed in college.

***Perseverance*** *is steady and continued action, usually over a long period, especially through difficulties and setbacks.*[1] There will be difficulties and challenges on your journey through college, but you will stay steady on the path as part of your noble plan.

***Flexibility*** *is the ability to adapt to new situations.* Being flexible also assures that you can bend (be stretched) without breaking. You will face many new and stressful situations. Being flexible (without being persuaded into activities that block your goal) allows you to learn and adapt while staying on your pathway.

---

1     *Encarta World English Dictionary* (1999), Anne Soukhanov, editor. St. Martin›s Press, s.v. "perseverance (*n.*)," "flexibility (n.)," and "determination (n.)."

***Determination*** *is firmness of purpose, a resolution to succeed.* Again, this trait helps you through the trials and struggles you will encounter in college. These problems aren't impossible roadblocks but challenges for you to surmount.

Being stubborn is sometimes considered unreasonably determined. Being rigid (inflexible) when stubborn is harmful. But, when you falter in perseverance and determination, sometimes a small dose of stubbornness gets you over that last bit of the challenge.

> *Prayer: Father, I know I will face challenges on my college journey. I pray you will guide me to have a noble plan and that my plan, in service to you, will achieve noble deeds. I already know I have a dose of stubbornness, but I pray you will grant me perseverance, flexibility, and determination to navigate my pathway through college.*

# BE STRONG AND COURAGEOUS

Be strong and very courageous. Be careful to obey all the law my servant Moses gave you; do not turn from it to the right or to the left, that you may be successful wherever you go.

**Joshua 1:7**

I once heard a parent remind their son as he left on a journey, "Remember who you are!" Your parent or guardian may have given you the same directive at some point in your life (maybe as you were leaving for college).

Of course, you know *who* you are, but you are being reminded to remember *whose* you are—the foundation of your upbringing, the *values* they taught you. Your parents, family, and loved ones want the best *for* you, but they also want the best *of* you. Just as Joshua reminded the Israelites to remember the law given to Moses by God, your parents want you to remember the virtues you have been taught:

- Be honest and trustworthy.
- Respect yourself and others.
- Demonstrate integrity (high moral principles) in all situations.
- Persevere through trials.
- Honor God and your family through your actions.

God loves you unconditionally. So does your family.

Your family wants you to succeed in college. (God does too.) Your family wants to be proud of your actions, and they will be thrilled when you graduate. God sees and knows everything you do. Your family won't see you as often and will have little knowledge of your behavior if you are living away from home. You, however, will know if your actions would be disappointing to them. Even if you are still living at home, your freedom as a college student is more extensive than when in high school.

Honor God and your family with your actions.

*Prayer: I pray for your guidance, Father, that*
*I may honor you and my family in all that I do.*

# A New Adventure— but You Are Not Alone

I will instruct you and teach you in the way you should go; I
will counsel you with my loving eye on you.

**Psalm 8:32**

You have worked hard academically and graduated high
school. This summer, you have made further preparation
for the giant step of being a college student. There will
be many more steps on your journey to college graduation and your career.

But, if it seems almost overwhelming, remember that
you only need to take one step at a time. However, you
need to keep stepping! Stay on the path to success on this
new journey.

The devotions that follow provide helpful advice in
many areas that will help you *Survive and Thrive* and
*Stay the Course* in this first, the most challenging, year of
college. While you may choose to read straight through
this book daily, please also keep handy the specific categories you should refer to as you need guidance:

- Developing and maintaining good relationships.
- Communicating with faculty.
- Developing effective study skills.
- Making wise decisions that lead to academic success.

- Avoiding temptations.
- Seeking help.
- Taking care of yourself physically and emotionally.
- Persevering through tough days.

As the summer ends and the fall semester begins, remember—**you are not alone**. God loves you and wants you to succeed on this new journey. He will guide your steps. He is always only a prayer away.

Your family and friends are praying for you as well.

*Prayer: This is it, God! I'm going to college! I'm ready, but I know there will be new challenges. I pray you will be with me and all new students. Help us be courageous, do our best, and most of all, help us seek your guidance on this journey.*

# Off to a good Start!

That important first week of classes.

## HOW NOT TO BEGIN

The instructor smiles in welcome as he enters the classroom, scanning the students already seated as they chat among themselves. Their conversation falters as they look at him expectantly. "You have a few minutes," he says, "it's fine to talk until class begins."

He peruses the members of the class, seeing apprehension in some faces. A few students sit silently, not joining in the conversation. Some of them are nervous, he thinks, remembering his freshman year.

Checking his watch, he calls for their attention, "Welcome to class!"

He explains a little about the class, called First Year Experience. "This course is designed to help you settle in to campus and guide you to develop skills and strategies to have a successful first year. This first semester, we'll be a community as we all work together to help you adapt to the academic challenges of college and adjust to being away from home."

After a brief explanation of the goals of the course, he introduces himself and asks students to do the same and share a little about themselves. Listening attentively, he writes a few notes about each student. He observes their physical features, matching faces to names in the quest to memorize names quickly.

About halfway through the class, a student barges in. Ignoring that class is already in session, he noisily makes his way to an empty seat, banging desks and bumping other students with his book bag. He laughs and blurts out, "I couldn't find the building."

Attempting to minimize the disruption, the instructor encourages the student whose introduction had been interrupted to continue. The tardy student attempts to talk to the person beside him. Murmuring an "excuse me," the professor moves in closer proximity to the rude student, asking him to be quiet. Several more reminders are needed before the student stops his disruptive behavior.

The student is tardy again for the next class period. The instructor addresses the issue with the young man after class, reminding him to be on time. The student shrugs his shoulders as he leaves the class, shouting to a friend to wait for him. The behavior repeats the next class period, and again, the student is reminded of the necessity to be on time. He rolls his eyes in response. The professor follows up with, "The door will be locked as soon as class begins. Be here on time."

The following class period, the instructor locks the classroom door one minute after the scheduled time to begin. Fifteen minutes later, the tardy student attempts to enter, then bangs on the door, shouting, "Let me in!"

The instructor responds, "Class started on time." The student pounds on the door and yells again before departing.

This example is based on an actual occurrence. Sadly, this student was not prepared for college, nor did he adapt his behavior to succeed. He wasn't ready for the commitment required to have a successful college experience. He did not develop the necessary traits of planning, organization, self-discipline, and a desire to succeed in the academic setting of college. This student did not successfully complete his first semester, having demonstrated the same type of behavior in all his other classes as well.

Beginning the semester with a great start will pave the wave for your success. The following segments in this section provide strategies for establishing a positive start to your school year and maintaining these good habits to achieve a positive outcome.

# GETTING OFF TO A GREAT START

There is a time for everything, and a season for every activity under the heavens.

**Ecclesiastes 3:1**

A good first week is a great jump-start to a successful first semester. You've done some preparation during the summer to help the first week of classes run smoothly.

Checklist before first class meeting:

- Do you know where your class is meeting? Check your schedule and search out each class listed (and the classroom) in advance. You don't want to be searching for your room at start time.
- Be sure you are in the right place. If you realize, when the instructor begins to speak, that you are in the wrong room, politely excuse yourself and find your correct class location.
- Listen carefully as the instructor introduces themself. What title does he/she expect to be called? It may be Mr., Mrs., or Ms., but more than likely, the professor will have a terminal degree (a PhD or an EdD), and you will need to address them as Doctor.
- As the instructor calls the roll, you may need to correct the pronunciation of your name or request

(politely and respectfully) to be called by a different name.

- Listen carefully to all information shared by the instructor during the first class meeting. Be especially attentive when the class syllabus is reviewed (see the next segment for more details about the importance of the syllabus).

*Prayer: The time is finally here! Classes are beginning. It's kind of scary. Actually, it's terrifying! I'm beginning the journey that leads to my future. My success depends on getting off to a good start. Father, I pray you will be with me and all our students and guide us on every aspect of the pathway you have planned.*

# THE SYLLABUS

I appeal to you, brothers and sisters, in the name of our Lord Jesus Christ, that all of you agree with one another in what you say and that there be no divisions among you, but that you be perfectly united in mind and thought.

**1 Corinthians 1:10**

The syllabus for each class is one of the most important documents of your educational experience. The syllabus outlines expectations for the class. Your instructor specifies the assignments, tasks, and behavior expected from you as a student. By signing up for the class, you *agree* to abide by the guidelines set forth in the syllabus and complete all assignments.

Thus, the syllabus acts as a contract, a written agreement, between you and the instructor. The actions needed to be successful in the class are specifically provided in the syllabus. As a participant in the class, you are accepting and agreeing to successfully complete those guidelines.

- Read the syllabus carefully.
- Read it again.
- Read it frequently throughout the semester.

**It is your responsibility to know what the assignments are and when they are due, the attendance**

**policy, the academic integrity code, and guidelines for use of technology in the classroom**. Students are accountable for *all* information included in the syllabus. Failure to consistently and correctly fulfill requirements for the course as outlined in the syllabus will cause your grade to suffer and could result in failure of the course.

If there are aspects of the syllabus that are not clear to you, **ask for clarification**. Ask questions about an assignment before it is due—not after you receive a poor grade on a task you didn't understand.

*Prayer: Father, the syllabus is an important and essential aspect of all my classes. Please help me read and follow the syllabus guidelines.*

# START THE SEMESTER WITH YOUR BEST EFFORT AND KEEP IT GOING!

Remember this: Whoever sows sparingly will also reap sparingly, and whoever sows generously will also reap generously.

**2 Corinthians 9:6**

Getting a good start is important for every semester, particularly in your first year. Give all you've got to do well in your first week of school and then keep giving your best effort consistently.

Establish good habits early on and maintain them.

- Attend all of your classes.
- Pay attention in class, listen carefully to all instructions, and take good notes.
- Avoid distractions in class (such as other students talking or doing non-academic actions).
- Avoid technology use (such as cell phones, laptops, or tablets) in class unless specifically stated and directed by the professor as needed for the class that day.
- Focus on the class you are in (don't work on tasks for a different class while attending another class).
- Complete required reading.
- Do all of your assignments.

- Not only do your assignments—give each task your best effort.
- Complete and turn in assignments on time, every time.
- Limit social time to after your schoolwork is done.
- Study as you go; don't depend on cramming for a test at the last minute.
- Complete papers or projects in advance to allow adequate time for proofreading and revisions.
- If your class has online assignments, check the site regularly and keep current on all required tasks.

Establishing and maintaining good habits will go far in helping you fulfill your plan to successfully complete your first semester and move forward toward graduation.

*Prayer: Father, I pray you'll help me get off to a good start in school and guide me to give my best effort in every class. Help me limit my social time or any distractions that keep me away from my academic studies.*

# CONSIDER EXTRA-CURRICULAR OPPORTUNITIES CAREFULLY

Where is the wise person? Where is the teacher of the law? Where is the philosopher of this age? Has not God made foolish the wisdom of the world? It is because of him that that you are in Christ Jesus, who has become for us wisdom from God—that is our righteousness, holiness and redemption.

**1 Corinthians 1:20, 30**

Your first week of school will be overwhelming. You'll be adjusting to a new environment away from home. You'll meet lots of new people—students, staff, and faculty. College requires many adaptations—different food, new relationships, more intense academic focus, and *lots* of decisions.

Early in the semester, focus on developing academic habits that will lead to your success in school. Remember, you are here to complete your degree and prepare for your future. Good study habits and a consistent focus on academic success are essential.

Are you a student-athlete? If so, you must balance sports and academic tasks so you will be successful in both.

You'll also need to make wise decisions about additional activities to participate in. It is important to be involved in campus life, develop social contacts, and have activities outside of attending classes and studying. However, keeping an appropriate balance is essential. Your college or university will have many extra-curricular activities from which to choose. Be wise in your decisions. Carefully consider the time commitment involved in the activities you select. Start with a few extra-curricular activities that will allow you to meet new people and make connections while leaving ample time for academic work.

*Prayer: Father, I want to do my best in school and make new friends and have new experiences. There's so much to choose from! Please help me choose wisely.*

# A New Thing!

See, I am doing a new thing! Now it springs up; do you not perceive it? I am making a way in the wilderness and streams in the wasteland.

**Isaiah 43:19**

You are definitely embarking on a "New Thing!"

The college/university experience is an amazing and thrilling adventure, an awesome experience, and a rewarding endeavor.

It can also be the most terrifying time of your life.

You may feel like a fish out of water, a lamb among wolves, or a waif abandoned among of strangers.

The good news is that God will make a way for you in this wilderness of new and confusing pathways.

You will survive, thrive and grow during your educational experience. That's not to say it will be easy. Sometimes you will feel you are lost in the wasteland, a solitary wanderer in the desert. But you are not alone. Most importantly, your Lord is with you. He will make pathways for you and guide you through trials, struggles, and scary times.

Sometimes, you will need to seek help from others. The pathway God shows you may be to talk to your professor about your poor performance in class, make an appointment to speak with a counselor about anxiety, visit the learning resource center to learn about study strategies, or go home for the weekend to speak with parents or a friend about your experiences. Many people are supporting you on this journey.

> *Prayer: Father, although sometimes I feel I'm alone in a wasteland, I know you are with me. I pray you will help me work hard and do my best; guide me through the tough times and show me the pathway for seeking help when I need it.*

# Making Wise Decisions

## GO TO CLASS OR . . .(A LESSON ON MAKING WISE DECISIONS)

The second-year students reported on their internship experiences, comparing locations, schedules, and interesting incidents that occurred during their weekly visits to their school placement.

"We had a lock-down drill in the middle of PE," exclaimed Patty. "The principal had told the teacher the safe place for any class in PE was the equipment room—no windows and a lock on the door. It's a tiny room to start with and stuffed with PE games and equipment. At the alarm, we were to take the students into that room and lock the door. We weren't to come out until the principal came to let us out." She waved her hands in agitation as her words tumbled out. "They were kindergarteners!"

A collective gasp filled the classroom.

"You were locked in a tiny room with kindergarteners?" Allie chuckled. "That must have been exciting."

"It was horrible," wailed Patty. "They forgot us. It was an hour before they let us out."

No more laughter. Wide eyes turned to the instructor as if seeking assurance they would not suffer this same calamity. Students had each been in their schools long enough to recognize the challenges of teaching those miniature bundles of energy. Squeezed into a tiny room with twenty squirming, squealing five-year-olds, *for an hour*, was beyond their ability to imagine, but they immediately expressed sympathy for Patty's plight.

The other students described their experiences, but none could top Patty's story—until it was Caleb's turn to report. "Uh . . ." His hands fidgeted on the table, and he didn't meet his instructor's gaze when she called on him. "Uh, I haven't been to my internship."

Another collective gasp and all eyes turned toward the teacher. What would she do?

The professor's sharp gaze rested on Caleb until he raised his head. She questioned, in a quiet voice that boded ill for the young man. "You haven't been to your school? This internship started three weeks ago."

Beads of sweat appeared on his forehead. "Um . . . well . . . ah . . . the time I'm scheduled to go is my only break from classes that day." He took a deep breath and met the professor's hard stare before he extended both hands. "So I ask myself the question," he gestured with one hand, "do I go to my internship?" He gestured with the other hand. "Or do I have lunch?"

A snort escaped from one student. She and other students covered their mouths to prevent laughter from escaping as they waited for the explosion they expected from their teacher. In an even softer voice that didn't conceal her annoyance and frustration, the professor said, "Caleb, that is the time you said you could be at your internship. **You chose that time**. Pack your lunch, take a snack, or . . ." She leaned forward and pinned him with her stare. "Go hungry, but if you intend to pass this class and continue toward graduation, GO TO YOUR INTERNSHIP."

Your class schedule or other required aspects of your academic life may not always be convenient for you. You may have to sacrifice a meal, some sleep, or social time. Commit your time first to school and all related academic responsibilities (completing assignments, studying, research, writing papers, internships, etc.). This doesn't mean you purposefully miss meals or sleep but is a reminder that, in college, you plan your daily schedule around your academic commitments.

# MAKE THE MOST OF OPPORTUNITY, BUT BE CAREFUL

Be very careful, then, how you live—not as unwise, but as wise, making the most of every opportunity, because the days are evil.

**Ephesians 5:15–16**

Being careful isn't just about avoiding harmful behaviors (alcohol, tobacco, drugs, risky behaviors, unsafe sex, etc.). Being careful also encompasses listening to the wisdom of your parents, family, faculty, and friends who care about you.

You'd probably be surprised if you knew the things your parents and mentors did when they were your age. When they caution you about certain behaviors, it's not because they never want you to have fun—it's because they care about your safety and about your ability to successfully complete your education and accomplish your goals in life. Listen to those who share wisdom with you about safety issues, study habits, and perseverance. And **remember, those who would entice you into behaviors that jeopardize your safety or threaten your success in school are not speaking to you with wisdom.**

Sadly, there is danger in our world and on your college campus. There will be times when you are tempted to fall into the pit of bad choices. You will want to go out with your friends instead of study; you may be tempted to cut classes because you stayed up too late the night before; you may label some classes (such as an internship) as unimportant; and others may encourage you to party and perhaps engage in dangerous behaviors. **Every class, assignment, internship, or other academic obligation is important.**

Stop and think before you indulge in dangerous, selfish, and irresponsible behavior. Remember your goals and make wise decisions.

> *Prayer: Father, sometimes I think my parents were born old and they know nothing about being young. Help me honor and respect my family and listen when they provide advice. Help me make the right decisions that will allow me to be successful.*

# DISCIPLINE

Endure hardship as discipline; God is treating you as his children. For what children are not disciplined by their father? No discipline seems pleasant at the time, but painful. Later on, however, it produces a harvest of righteousness and peace for those who have been trained by it.

**Hebrews 12:7, 11**

You've encountered various forms of discipline in your earlier life from parents, teachers, coaches, etc. Discipline isn't just punishment but involves teaching, learning, and a change of behavior if needed. College will be no exception to discipline, although much of it will be your decision.

Self-discipline is a vital part of your successful journey to complete your education. There will be times you want to blow off an assignment, skip class, or even quit school.

*You* will be the reason you don't give up. That's not to say your teachers and family don't have any influence. They are powerful advocates for you. They will encourage you. They want you to succeed. But, ultimately, the decision to attend all your classes, spend adequate time completing assignments, study effectively for tests and exams, and be diligent in all aspects of schooling is your responsibility.

This is where your self-discipline must guide you. It's hard and often unpleasant to force ourselves to achieve when we're tired, struggling, and don't always understand what we need to do. But your determination will produce a harvest as you persevere to successfully complete your college work.

Go to class. Keep up with your assignments. Seek help from family, professors, tutors, or student support services as needed. Your efforts will be blessed.

*Prayer: Father, I'm used to discipline, but one of the joys of independence is not having someone tell me what to do, isn't it? I may need some help with self-discipline. Please guide me to do my best and ask for help when needed.*

## SEEK THE LORD

How can a young person stay on the path of purity? By living according to your word. I will seek you with all my heart; do not let me stray from your commands. I have hidden your word in my heart that I might not sin against you.

**Psalm 119:9–11**

You may have an established faith in God. Perhaps you've been active in your church and youth group. You may be a veteran of numerous mission trips. If so, that's awesome!

You may be a new traveler with Jesus, still in the early stages of your Christian walk.

Or perhaps this book was a gift to you, and you do not yet know Jesus.

No matter the stage of your faith, I'm praying for you. I pray you can stay on the path of purity—that your faith will grow stronger with each step of your college journey and that the Holy Scripture will be your companion. I pray you will make friends who share your faith in Jesus and you will be a good example for others and they for you.

It may be easy for you to find Christian friends on campus, or it may be a challenge. Perhaps your campus has a chaplain or pastor. He or she can be a spiritual leader and mentor for you. Hopefully, there are Christian organizations you may join so that you have a support group of fellow believers. Don't give up as you seek friends that offer help and encouragement in your faith.

*Prayer: Father, I pray I will seek you with all my heart. Please strengthen my faith and show me the path I need to take in obedience and service to you. Please send me spiritual mentors and friends to support me on my journey and guide me to be a good role model for my friends and classmates.*

## Gaining Wisdom and Prudence

I, wisdom, dwell together with prudence; I possess knowledge and discretion.

**Proverbs 8:12**

Prudence can be defined as being careful and having good sense. Another characteristic of prudence is forethought—thinking about something before you do it.

Good advice.

You will be faced with a lot of decisions while in college. Examples?

- Choosing your friends.
- Setting your schedule (when to go out, study, sleep, etc.).
- Selecting your social activities—when, what, where, and with whom.
- Clubs and activities in which to participate.

These are somewhat benign choices, not particularly dangerous (although they can be). The decisions you make in these categories will certainly affect your ability to succeed in college. Be wise and prudent; use your good sense in making these decisions. **If an activity or a person interferes with your ability to be successful in**

**school, your good sense should tell you to limit contact with this person or activity.**

Other behaviors may have more serious consequences:

- Do you take your studies seriously? Are you doing your best or blowing off your classes and failing to do homework?
- Are you indulging in unhealthy behaviors, such as drugs, alcohol, or unprotected sex?
- Do you spend beyond your budget?
- Are you making healthy nutrition choices, exercising regularly, and getting enough sleep?

Remember, **be prudent and wise; think before you make a decision**. Is this action going to support me on my journey to be successful in college or will this decision bring harm to me or others?

> *Prayer: Father, in the past others have made most of my decisions for me. Being able to choose for myself is not as easy as I thought. I pray you will grant me wisdom so that I will make the right choices. Please help me avoid risky behaviors and temptations.*

## Choosing How to Conform

Do not conform to the pattern of this world, but be transformed by the renewing of your mind. Then you will be able to test and approve what God's will is—his good pleasing and perfect will.

**Romans 12:2**

***Conform*** means to behave acceptably, follow a certain standard, or be made similar.[2]

You've probably conformed for all your life; your parents and mentors had certain rules, guidelines, and principles they expected you to follow. In school, you were expected to conform to another set of established rules. The same situation exists in the job setting as well. Most likely, there will never be a time when we aren't conforming to someone's guidelines.

But Paul's admonition is reminding us to always use the standard of God's guidelines to set our own actions. College is an ideal place to "renew our minds" because you are continuously absorbing new knowledge and engaging in new experiences. But it is your choice how you conform. You will be encouraged to spread your wings and fly—to be creative and embrace new opportunities. At the same time, you are expected to conform to

---

2    *Encarta World English Dictionary* (1999), Anne Soukhanov, editor. St. Martin's Press, s.v. "conform (v.)."

university policies and an established set of social guidelines. There will also be the desire to rebel against previously held convictions as being too strict, outdated, or irrelevant. When these temptations arise, it is time to turn to God and seek His guidance in selecting actions that will embrace your new growth, without causing harm to yourself, your family, or your future career aspirations.

> *Prayer: Father, as I set out on this new journey to grow and learn, I pray that you will guide me to seek your will and keep me on the path to your "good, pleasing and perfect will."*

# KEEP YOUR CONNECTION TO HOME

My people will live in peaceful dwelling places, in secure homes, in undisturbed places of rest.

**Isaiah 32:18**

If you live on campus, particularly if far from home, your trips to visit family will be infrequent. When you go, you'll discover things are different. But it won't be home that has changed—it will be you.

As you grow, mature, and spread your wings to leave the nest (home), you will have a different perspective on life and home. It isn't that you will love your family less, but other priorities will pull at your time.

Continue to nurture the loving relationship with your family as you balance your establishment of independence. Your family will adjust to the maturing adult you are becoming.

Even if you live close enough to go home every weekend or you are a commuter, you and your family will notice changes. Patience, tolerance, and compassion are needed to accept that your relationships are changing, not for the worse but changing nonetheless. Establish your independence, but do so in a loving and kind manner that doesn't exclude your family from your life.

Continue to visit as often as you are able. Recognize your family is always going to be a special part of your life. Rejoice in your growth and maturity as your wings become stronger, enabling you to soar away from the nest, but return often to your family.

> *Prayer: Father, there are so many challenges in being away from home. Sometimes I miss being a child and crawling into my mom's lap and telling her all my frustrations. I know I'm on the way to being an adult, being independent, and making my own decisions. Help me to always honor my family and show my love for them.*

# Resisting Temptation

Be Prepared—Because Temptations Will Come

## LEARNING TO SAY NO (EVEN IF IT MEANS GIVING UP SOMETHING GOOD)

A sob erupted, and tears streamed down her face.

Taken aback by the burst of emotion, her advisor reached into his desk drawer, grabbed a box, and extended the much-needed tissues to the student. "Take your time," he murmured to the student, unable to understand any of the jumble of words babbling forth.

After a few minutes, Annie murmured, "I'm so sorry." She gulped for air to control her weeping. "I just had to talk with you."

"I've got some time before my next class. What's wrong?"

"I'm failing anatomy," she wailed. Another round of tears flowed.

"We're just getting started in the semester. Isn't it too soon to tell that you're failing?"

Annie swiped at her nose. "We just got our first test back. I made 52 on it!"

"Sometimes, it takes the first test to understand the kind of tests your instructor gives and the type of questions being asked," her advisor responded. "You learn from your mistakes on the first test to help you get better on the later ones."

"I've never been good at science. It's just too hard. We have to memorize all the bones and muscles, all the body systems and how they work, and so much more." Fresh tears leaked from her eyes. "I can't remember all that stuff. I need to change my major!"

"Slow down, Annie. It isn't the time to change your major just because you did poorly on your first test." He passed the dejected girl another tissue. "Talk to me about how you prepared for the test. Do you take notes in class?"

"I try to, but I can't keep up, and I don't understand the material. My notes are just a jumble of words that don't make sense to me."

"Does your instructor provide a study guide? When did you start to study for the test?"

"Yes, we have a study guide, but I didn't have time to complete it. I studied for hours on the night before the test."

"Tell me a little more about your schedule. I know your classes since I'm your advisor, and I know you have soccer. Does the team practice every day?"

Annie sagged in her chair. "Yes, except on Sundays, but even then, we practice if we have a bad game during the week and need extra work."

"Why didn't you have time to complete the study guide?" her advisor asked.

Annie stared down at her clenched hands. "Well, we had a sorority meeting three times this past week because we're working on a special service project. I had a paper due in religion class and a test in history." She put her face in her hands and mumbled, "I can't keep up."

"It sounds like your schedule is very busy, but we can work on some planning to give you more time. Have you talked to your sorority about needing more study time?"

She lifted her head. "I'm afraid they will throw me out if I don't go to all the work sessions."

Her advisor shook his head. "They want you to be successful in school and make good grades. Although service is a very important part of their mission, they don't want it to interfere with your ability to get your schoolwork done. It's important to your sorority that you do well academically. You will need to ask them about cutting back on your volunteer hours until you catch up on your schoolwork and have a more manageable schedule. Since this is your soccer season, you should ask them to let you complete all your volunteer hours in the spring."

Annie sat a little straighter. "I hadn't thought of that. You think they will?"

"If you explain you need more time for academics, they will understand. You can't give up soccer since you're on a scholarship, but your sorority should be willing to work with you on this. Right now, you have too many obligations. You're going to have to give up something."

A glimmer of hope shone through the tears. "I didn't think I could, but it's a good idea if my sorority will let me do that."

Leaning forward to rest his hands on his desk, her advisor asked, "What else can you give up to allow for more study time? Are you spending too much time in social activities?"

Annie pondered the question. "I hadn't thought about that either, but I've been hanging out with some of the team in the evenings, just talking, trying to unwind after a hard day."

Her advisor nodded. "You need some of that as a stress reliever, but if you make that time shorter, you would have extra study time."

Annie nodded. "And the time I have between classes, I could go somewhere and study instead of talking to friends."

The professor leaned back in his chair. "Now you're on the right track. Sometimes we have to say no to things we want to do to have time to complete what we must do. Use those extra minutes during the day to study and review. Go over the notes you take in class when they are fresh in your mind. You can fill in some of the gaps before you forget what the instructor said. Try to review your notes every day to help you remember what will be on the next test."

"And another thing," his gaze grew stern, "don't wait until the night before the test to begin studying. Set aside some time every day the week before your test to study."

Annie nods, then frowns. "But what about anatomy? It's too hard!" Her eyes glistened with renewed tears.

"Well, I have some ideas about that too . . ."

# THERE WILL BE TEMPTATIONS

So, if you think you are standing firm, be careful that you don't fall! No temptation has overtaken you except what is common to mankind. And God is faithful; he will not let you be tempted beyond what you can bear. But when you are tempted, he will also provide a way out so that you can endure it.

**I Corinthians 10:12–13**

College is a whole new world, whether you live at home and commute, take online classes, or reside on campus. Temptations will be greater, of course, if you are away from home. Freedom is a stimulating concept—with it comes a plethora of new opportunities (that's what college is all about), but with those new opportunities are a multitude of choices.

- Do I choose to study tonight or go out with my friends?
- Do I go to my 8:00 a.m. class or sleep in?
- Do I hang out with this group because they are so much fun or go to my study group?
- Do I take higher risks, such as using alcohol or drugs?

You will have a surge of adrenalin at your new freedom. Your parents or guardian will no longer be reminding you to get up on time, study, and not stay out too late. Temptations will attack you daily. In future segments, we will discuss specific activities and strategies you can use to resist succumbing to harmful temptations. But remember, you have One who is faithful, who will never let you down; He will listen when you cry out for strength and courage. God is trustworthy and faithful.

> *Prayer: Father, I know you are always faithful and will hear me when I cry out to you for help. Please guide me to call on you in my time of need.*

# BE ALERT

---

Be alert and of sober mind. Your enemy the devil prowls around like a roaring lion looking for someone to devour. Resist him, standing firm in the faith, because you know the family of believers throughout the world is undergoing the same kind of sufferings.

**1 Peter 5:8–9**

The devil searches for our weaknesses. He'd like nothing better than for you to succumb to doubts and fears. He may use others to influence you into destructive behaviors that can destroy your future plans.

Your primary goals at college should be to learn as much as possible and complete your degree in preparation for a rewarding career that contributes to society. Of course, there are secondary goals, such as being a successful athlete, having new and rewarding experiences, and making lifelong friends. If you have questionable purposes in mind, such as indulging in illegal, dangerous, or other risky behaviors, the outcome will be disastrous for your future. Some actions can lead to expulsion from the institution or cause you to fail courses. A "good time" for the moment can lead to the dousing of your future career dreams.

Be alert! Guard against those who attempt to pull you away from your dreams. Gratification for the moment is not worth the loss of your future. Be alert for self-doubt. Feelings of anxiety or depression frequently happen with the pressures of college. Stay in prayer for guidance. Seek the company of believers as a support group. Search for help through support services at your institution when doubt, fear, or depression are too fierce for you to handle.

*Prayer: Please help me stay in a close relationship with you, my Father. You are my anchor in the storm.*

# TAKE THE NARROW ROAD

Enter through the narrow gate. For wide is the gate and broad is the road that leads to destruction, and many enter through it. But small is the gate and narrow the road that leads to life, and only a few find it.

**Matthew 7:13–14**

College is a time of many "firsts." Often, it's the first time you are away from home for extended periods. While you may have dealt with various temptations in high school, college life brings a whole new set of enticements. For the first time, you'll be primarily on your own, with very little parental supervision. You'll be setting your own schedule and making decisions that will determine if you succeed in college.

Parents or guardians will not be screening your acquaintances or making recommendations about friends. It will be your decision if you choose the "party crowd," which has only one focus—having a good time—or the more studious group, with people who have come to college to receive an education to benefit their future. Choose your friends wisely. Avoid those who will tempt you into high-risk behaviors under the guise of "having fun." Surround yourself with students willing to study, attend class, and complete assignments. There will still be time for fun when homework is finished.

*Prayer: Father, I pray you will guide me in the selection of my college friends; that you will send me a roommate, classmates, and friends who are encouragers. Please guide us to do our best. Help us find the path leading to life, not destruction.*

# RESISTING TEMPTATION

Submit yourselves, then, to God. Resist the devil, and he will flee from you.

**James 4:7**

College offers many opportunities—learning and preparing for a career, making new and life-long friends, and maturing and gaining independence.

As with any new stage in our life where independence is within our grasp, temptations emerge from every direction. As a young adult, you are now making major decisions that will affect you for a lifetime. Your success or failure in college depends on your ability to focus on your goal to do your best and finish your degree.

No matter how well or poorly you are prepared for college work, there will be times when you will be challenged academically and consider giving up and quitting school.

No matter how self-disciplined you believe yourself to be, there will be times when you want to blow off an assignment, skip class because you stayed up too late the previous night, or go out with friends instead of studying for a test. These are the times when you need to pray for strength to do what you *ought* to do instead of what you *want* to do.

Remember, the devil wants us to fail. The devil thrives on our weaknesses and whispers doubt into our consciousness, telling us that having a little fun won't cause us any problems.

You cannot avoid being tempted, but you can keep from giving in. When temptation beckons and you are unsure how to resist, cry out to the Lord and ask for help. God wants you to succeed.

> *Prayer: Father, I want to be successful in college. But I want to have some fun too. Help me to know what is harmful and what is beneficial.*

## STAND FIRM IN THE FAITH

Be on your guard; stand firm in the faith; be people of courage; be strong. Do everything in love.

**1 Corinthians 16:13–14**

We spoke earlier about temptations. One of the realities of temptation is that it is always around. Each day brings new thoughts and situations that threaten to derail you from your goal to give your best to your college education.

Be on guard!

- Are you tempted to skip class, cheat or do less than your best?
- Are you being encouraged to party or use alcohol and drugs?
- Are you tempted to turn in sub-par work because you've procrastinated?
- Have social activities interfered with study time?
- Are you overwhelmed and want to quit?

We are all tempted—every day—to turn aside from challenging goals and take the easier path. We are not promised an easy journey, but we are promised that our Lord will help us on the journey to serve Him.

"Come to me, all you who are weary and burdened, and I will give you rest. Take my yoke upon you and learn from me, for I am gentle and humble in heart, and you will find rest for your soul. For my yoke is easy and my burden is light."

**Matthew 11:28–30**

When you feel the urge to do less than your best or to participate in activities that can threaten your goals, turn to your support group for encouragement. And, most importantly, seek God's strength to stand firm in your faith.

*Prayer: Father, I know you are only a prayer away. But sometimes, I do things I shouldn't on the spur of the moment. I forget to call on you for help. Please protect me, even when I don't remember to ask.*

# Relationships

Getting along Well with Faculty, Staff, and other Students

## RELATIONSHIPS AND COMMUNICATION ARE IMPORTANT

Relationships can be positive but also painful, no matter your age or whether you are a student or a teacher. But *all* relationships are important. Consider these short examples of faculty and student interactions:

After a student was privately[3] chastised for not following directions on an online assignment, he complained to the Dean of Student Affairs. When the instructor tried to clarify the misunderstanding and apologize for what the student perceived as a harsh response by the teacher, the student refused to accept the apology. Even though

---

3    Any negative feedback or potentially controversial discussions between faculty and student or student to faculty should occur in private. An instructor should never criticize students in the presence of other students, nor should a student negatively criticize a faculty member in the presence of others. The rule of thumb is, "Praise in public, criticize in private."

the student was at fault for failing to complete the assignment correctly, he refused to accept any responsibility for his error, instead choosing to blame the faculty member.

Following a discussion of her performance in the student-teacher setting and recommendations of actions that could improve her teaching, the student became angry, yelling, "You're always picking on me" and ran from the room. This student complained to her advisor and an uncomfortable meeting ensued, with the student unloading her frustration on the confused professor while the advisor attempted to mediate. The professor defended her expectations that all students in the class were expected to perform at a high level. A rocky relationship continued throughout the semester.

A student barges into his instructor's office, attempting to intimidate her with curses and threats over a poor grade on an assignment. Only a call to security resulted in his departure.

The above examples illustrate inappropriate interactions between students and faculty. Such incidents usually occur when students are angry and upset about perceived mistreatment. There are more mature ways to handle these situations. You will find recommendations for student/faculty interactions in the following category of devotions, which focus on relationships. Keep in mind that everyone makes mistakes and none of us is perfect. When we are frustrated and angry, we are apt to say and do things we may regret later. At these times, a dose of patience and tolerance can help calm the situation.

In college, students interact with each other (roommates, friends, classmates, etc.) and with faculty and staff. All of these relationships are important and each is an essential part of your college experience. Maturity, respect, and consideration are necessary to maintain appropriate relationships. In the following section, you will find information to help guide your relationships and appropriate strategies to utilize to resolve conflict.

Fortunately for all of us, not all communication between faculty and students is antagonistic. An excellent student emailed her instructor following the posting of grades. "Why did I receive an *F* in your class?"

*What?* This star student didn't make an *F*. However, when the professor checked the posted grades, an *F* was listed. It was a mistake on the instructor's part, which he immediately rectified and responded to her with an apology. The student handled the situation with respect and maturity, reaching out to her professor first, with no accusations or volatility. She recognized that professors are human and sometimes make mistakes and the instructor owned his mistake (a trait all faculty and students should possess).

# BE CAREFUL NOT TO JUDGE

Do not judge, and you will not be judged. Do not condemn and you will not be condemned. Forgive, and you will be forgiven.

**Luke 6:37**

Jesus is speaking to His disciples, reminding them (and us) how we should treat others. In the same chapter of Luke (vs. 41–42), Jesus questions: **"Why do you look at the speck of sawdust in your brother's eye and pay no attention to the plank in your own eye? How can you say to your brother, 'Brother let me take the speck out of your eye,' when you yourself fail to see the plank in your own eye?"**

This is one of life's most challenging lessons—learning not to judge people for what we perceive as their faults before we examine our own limitations. It's far easier to look at others and question what they should (or shouldn't) be doing.

College offers a cross-section of life for you to make hasty judgments. It becomes easy to develop feelings of frustration and anger when you believe your needs are not being met. You may feel the urge to judge other students, your instructors, members of clubs or teams of which you are a part, campus support personnel, library and food service staff, the college administrators, etc. In this section, we examine relationships you will form as part of your college experience and discuss strategies you can use to keep these relationships functional, meaningful, and amiable.

> *Prayer: Father, there are so many people on campus I need to work with. Some haven't been friendly or helpful. I pray you will grant me the ability to reach out to those who will guide and assist me in my college experience, and we will be kind and courteous in all our interactions.*

# BE TOLERANT

We who are strong ought to bear with the failings of the weak and not to please ourselves. Each of us should please our neighbors for their good, to build them up.

**Romans 15:1–2**

You've already noticed there are many imperfect people in the world. College is no different. You will meet other students whom you find irritating. You'll have instructors you don't like. You may have a roommate who drives you crazy. There will be times when others are rude or treat you unfairly.

Yesterday's devotion discussed the importance of not judging others. This is a critical component of learning tolerance. There are likely thousands of people on your college campus when the numbers of students, faculty, and staff are considered. Each of these individuals is a unique person with their own personality. We are all different. But we're also very similar. **One common goal shared by all on a college campus is every person wants students to succeed in achieving their educational goals.**

That doesn't mean that college will be easy. On the contrary, completing your education may be one of the most challenging experiences of your life. This quest for success can make emotions run high and tempers ignite on a short fuse. Thus, the need for tolerance becomes apparent. Others will make mistakes and may not live up to your expectations, but we should be patient, understanding, and tolerant of the shortcomings of others. You will appreciate being given the same consideration.

One note of warning: tolerance from an instructor does not extend to students who are not attending class, not completing work on time, not giving their best effort, or are exhibiting inappropriate behavior. To expect tolerance and understanding from your teachers, you must do your part to give 100 percent effort.

*Prayer: Father, I'm thankful you have patience, compassion, and tolerance for me. Please help all of us here on campus to have that same understanding and caring attitude for each other.*

# SEEK PEACE

Turn from evil and do good; seek peace and pursue it.

**Psalm 34:14**

The above Scripture is not meant to label you as evil if you're struggling to get along with someone, but Jesus reminds us of the importance of loving each other (part of seeking peace).

Love the Lord your God with all your heart and with all your soul and with all your mind. This is the first and greatest commandment. And the second is like it: Love your neighbor as yourself.

**Matthew 22:37–39**

Who is your neighbor? In college or university, your neighbor is anyone with whom you come in contact—fellow students, faculty, staff, and community.

Sometimes, although we've given our best effort, we still struggle to get along with someone. Your conflict may be with a peer (another student) or someone in a faculty or staff position. Finding a favorable solution to a conflict in either of these situations is important, but the strategies are different.[4]

---

4    Conflict with faculty or staff—next page.

With a peer, ask yourself, *"What's my role in this disagreement? What can I do to ease the conflict?"* Even if you view the other person as being at fault, you can still seek peace. The most challenging solution may be accepting the apology you never receive, which means forgiving the person, even if they never acknowledge their part in the conflict. As adults, we can be polite and respectful in all situations. Even disagreement with another's point of view can be expressed in a respectful manner.

> *Prayer: Father, it is challenging being away from home, in a new environment, with so many people. I have so many tasks to accomplish I'm sometimes overwhelmed and anxious. Please help me be kind and respectful to others in all situations.*

## Communicating with Faculty and Staff in Challenging Situations

Let everyone be subject to the governing authority, for there is no authority except that which God has established. The authorities that exist have been established by God.

**Romans 13:1**

Yesterday's devotion focused on seeking peace (resolving conflicts) with your peers. Today, we examine communicating with faculty and staff when you have a concern. This can be a more challenging situation since these people are not your peers, but are in a position of authority. Your approach to resolving issues is different.

Examples of potential concerns or conflict may include:

- A grade you disagree with.
- An assignment you don't understand.
- Miscommunication between you and the faculty or staff member.
- An instance in which you feel you have been treated unfairly.
- Instructor not providing feedback promptly.
- Faculty or staff not returning your calls or emails.

In these situations, it is not appropriate to confront the faculty member or staff in class or when he/she is engaged in another task. Ask for an appointment. Discuss your concerns calmly and respectfully, asking what you can do to rectify the situation. If you have, in any way, contributed to the possible conflict, apologize before expressing your concerns or asking for grace (such as an opportunity to make up an assignment you did not understand).

Continue to be respectful, even if the situation is not resolved as you wish. Remember, words once spoken can never be taken back. The next two segments provide information about how to proceed if you feel the conflict has not been resolved.

*Prayer: Father, talking to those in authority can be downright scary! Please help me be brave but polite whenever such situations arise.*

# FOLLOWING CHAIN OF COMMAND

And he asked them, "Whose image is this? And whose
    inscription?"
"Caesar's," they replied.
Then he said to them, "So give back to Caesar what is
Caesar's, and to God what is God's."

**Matthew 22:20–21**

If you've had a conflict with a member of the faculty
or staff at your university, met with them to discuss the
situation, and haven't been able to resolve the conflict,
what should you do?

Important first steps:

- Pray for guidance.
- Gather relevant information about the situation.
- Reflect honestly on the situation.
- To organize your thoughts, write a summary.

Ask yourself:

- Have I done all I can to resolve the situation?
- Have I met face-to-face with the professor or
  staff member to discuss the issue?
- If an online class, have I emailed the instructor?

- Have I been courteous and respectful in all inter-actions?
- Have I followed through with another request if I didn't receive an answer from my first attempt?

If you've not been able to resolve the issue, your next approach is to speak to the faculty or staff member's **direct** supervisor.

- Again, be certain that you have done all that is possible to resolve the situation before approaching an administrator.
- Follow the proper chain of command. It is not appropriate for you to contact the president of your university to discuss a faculty/student conflict.
- Contact the immediate supervisor first and request an appointment to meet. Be well-organized, calm, and courteous as you present your information.
- This initial supervisor will inform you about how to proceed if you wish to continue up the chain of command with your complaint.

*Prayer: I pray I will have good relation-ships with faculty and staff. But, if something should happen, please guide me in the pro-cess of conflict resolution.*

# WHEN YOU THINK NO ONE IS LISTENING—PERSIST

Then Jesus said to her, "Woman, you have great faith! Your request is granted." And her daughter was healed at that moment.

**Matthew 15:28**

There's a problem you can't resolve with a faculty or staff member. You've met with this person and shared your concern, but the issue continues. What is your next step?

Don't give up. Be persistent. Maintain a polite and mature attitude. Continue to be respectful to this person in all communication. Work hard in the class (or whatever setting) to complete your best work.

However, if your concern continues and the situation is serious enough that it affects your ability to succeed, it may be time to speak to someone else. Your academic advisor can offer advice about how to proceed. Student support services or a college counselor may also share some wisdom that will help resolve the situation. If you feel you have exhausted all efforts of resolution, it may be time to contact the immediate supervisor of the faculty or staff member.

Information you will need:

- Name of the department in which the faculty or staff member is located.
- Head of the department.
- A thorough yet concise description of the situation. Include only relevant facts (saying the person doesn't like you is opinion, not fact).
- List attempts you've made to rectify the situation (dates of meetings and actions you tried).
- Make an appointment with the immediate supervisor—do not skip to the dean or president. Go through the proper chain of command.
- Be respectful and polite in the meeting; present only facts (not hearsay or gossip).

*Prayer: Please grant me open and positive communication with my superiors. But, if I need help, please guide me on the path I should go.*

# DO NO HARM

Jesus replied: "Love the Lord your God with all your heart and with all your soul and with all your mind. This is the first and greatest commandment. And the second is like it, Love your neighbor as yourself."

**Matthew 22: 36–39**

You will have many "neighbors" on your college campus. Faculty, staff, and students are your neighbors. Basic universal guidelines include:

- Be polite and respectful in all interactions.
- Maintain appropriate respect and attitude toward faculty and staff.
- Demonstrate a positive attitude.
- Be a good role model (demonstrate behaviors that contribute to the successful completion of academic goals).

So what is with the "Do No Harm" title of this devotion?

In this case, I'm not speaking of active shooters, a flu epidemic, or a COVID-19 pandemic, and I pray that you never face such tragedies. My focus is on your behavior and how you can have a positive impact on your neighbors on campus.

- Avoid behaviors that are dangerous to yourself or others.

- Don't encourage your peers to participate in unsafe behaviors, such as alcohol or drug abuse, reckless driving, or any action that could bring harm.

- Remember and abide by your school's academic honor code. Don't cheat or assist anyone else in cheating.

- Be an encourager—everyone feels overwhelmed at times. You can help by offering positive encouragement (and avoiding negative comments).

- Report negative behavior: underage drinking, use of drugs, crimes, and suspicions of dangerous or erratic behavior. It is not tattling when you are trying to protect others.

- If your peers are struggling in any way (substance abuse, depression, severe emotional disturbance), seek help from support staff. Your intervention could save someone's life.

*Prayer: Father, I pray you will be with each person here—and you will guide us to always be good neighbors.*

# WHEN TO TELL

Have nothing to do with the fruitless deeds of darkness, but rather expose them.

**Ephesians 5:11**

No one likes a tattle-tale. We learned that in elementary school. But, even at a young age, we knew it was important to tell when danger was involved.

Sadly, there is still danger in our world. There will be potential hazards on and around your college campus. Some of these dangers are obvious and easy for you to report to authorities. These might include someone breaking into vehicles in the parking lot, a stranger on campus intent on harm, or any illegal activity.

But some things may be harder to report. What happens when you witness underage drinking? What if you are being pushed to use illegal drugs? What do you do when a fraternity or sorority initiation involves actions that are dangerous? What should you do when you witness cheating?

Your first instinct may be to say nothing because you don't want to be a tattle-tale and you don't want to get anyone in trouble. However, some of these issues can be a matter of life and death. Activities that can cause harm to others should be reported immediately. On a college campus, you are a community, and it's vital to do all you can to keep all members of your community safe.

> *Prayer: Father, I pray you will protect us. I pray for the safety of all students, faculty, and staff. I pray we will all act with responsibility and integrity and we won't cause harm to one another. If we witness something dangerous, please give us the courage to tell those in charge. Help us do our best to keep each other safe.*

# WHOLESOME TALK

Do not let any unwholesome talk come out of your mouths, but only what is helpful for building others up according to their needs, that it may benefit those who listen.

**Ephesians 4:29**

The Bible tells us the tongue is a dangerous part of our body. Our tongue is hard to control and tempted to evil.

But no human being can tame the tongue. It is a restless evil, full of deadly poison.

**James 3:8**

We all know words can hurt. We've been on the receiving end of verbal abuse and have likely been the ones delivering painful words on occasion. Sometimes words pop from our mouths like dangerous darts that pierce the heart of the hearer. We can seek God's help in learning to control the hurtful language that comes from our mouths.

You will be in contact with many people on your college journey. Sometimes there will be conflict situations. We experience frustration and anger if we feel mistreated and may be tempted to strike out with words in retaliation. But, whatever the situation, we need to think before we speak:

- Should I say anything?
- Is the comment or response I'm about to make kind?
- Are my words uplifting or am I putting someone down?
- Am I speaking in respect and love or with anger?
- Are my words beneficial to the other person?
- Should I just be quiet?

*Prayer: Father, I know my tongue and voice can be a weapon of pain if I'm not careful. Please help me be polite, kind, and thoughtful in my interactions with others. And, if I'm really upset and angry, please guide me to think before I speak and control myself to avoid harsh words.*

# Be Kind

Get rid of all bitterness, rage and anger, brawling and slander, along with every form of malice. Be kind and compassionate to one another, forgiving each other, just as in Christ God forgave you.

**Ephesians 4:31–32**

A college campus resembles a very large family of unique individuals. There will be times of happiness and joy when everyone gets along and loves everyone else. But peace and harmony don't always last. The negative traits Paul mentions above rear their ugly heads, and conflict and strife result. We sometimes become frustrated and angry and are tempted to treat others in ways that are not kind or considerate.

Just as within your smaller family circle, it's important to exhibit kindness and compassion for your fellow students, campus staff, and faculty. As imperfect humans, we struggle with the concept of being kind all the time, but with God's help, we can make a good effort.

We can choose how we react to situations and circumstances. If another person is rude to us, if we're frustrated, if we believe we've been insulted, or if our feelings have been hurt, **we decide how we will respond**. We can choose an alternative response instead of anger.

When confronted with conflict, we can excuse our-selves and walk away. We can respond with kindness instead of anger to one who has hurt us. We can make the choice to forgive rather than escalate the situation by reacting with frustration. We can choose compassion rather than retaliation.

We can choose to be kind.

*Prayer: Father, I want to be kind and com-passionate, but you know it's sometimes hard to control myself when I'm frustrated and upset. I need your help! Please guide me to act with love and kindness in my relation-ships with others.*

# BE AN ENCOURAGER

Therefore encourage one another and build each other up,
just as in fact you are doing.

**1 Thessalonians 5:11**

We all benefit from encouragement, and college is no exception. In fact, college is stressful enough that *lots* of encouragement is needed. You'll likely receive encouragement from your family and close friends. But what about on campus?

It is important for you to **be an encourager**. Other students in your classes, your roommate, and new friends you meet on campus will greatly benefit from your encouragement.

Everyone has rough days and challenging tasks that threaten to defeat us. College will create trials, stress, and obstacles for you and other students. Offering support to others in need not only benefits them but you as well. Having a positive outlook helps us spread hope to others and receive encouragement from them in return.

Now we ask you, brothers and sisters, to acknowledge those who work hard among you, who care for you in the Lord and who admonish you. Hold them in the highest regard in love because of their work. Live in peace with each other.

**1 Thessalonians 5:12–13**

And sometimes, we need that "kick in the pants." Encouragement goes far, and we should give it freely, but we should be able to give and receive constructive criticism as well. Your friends, your roommate, and you may need a "wake-up call" if you aren't giving your best effort to your studies.

Remember, if you need to admonish (offer constructive criticism or correction) or if you are on the receiving end of constructive criticism, give and respond with kindness and respect.

*Prayer: Father, help me be a good friend and encourager. Help me look for the best in others. And, if I or others need correction, help us give and accept with respect and love.*

# SEEK THE PATH OF WISDOM

Wisdom will save you from the ways of wicked men, from men whose words are perverse, who have left the straight paths to walk in dark ways, who delight in doing wrong and rejoice in the perverseness of evil.

**Proverbs 2:12–14**

Life would be easier if there were no wicked or evil people to lead us astray. In the college environment, you will encounter those who would entice you into making decisions that may be harmful to you. The good news is that you have control of your behavior.

**You can say no.**

How will you know if you are being encouraged into harmful actions?

Involvement in illegal drugs or underage drinking is not only dangerous to your health and well-being, it's against the law. Two good reasons to say no.

Hanging out or partying with friends (even if no illegal behavior is going on) instead of studying is detrimental to your success in college. Be sure you are prepared in all classes before planning social time. There will be times when you should say no to your friends.

The desire for sexual intimacy is a natural part of life. Abstinence is the most effective way to protect you from sexually transmitted diseases/infections (STDs, STIs) and unplanned pregnancy. A discussion of intimacy should be a part of your relationships to make your feelings clear in advance. It's okay to say no to sexual relationships.

> *Prayer: Father God, I've looked forward to being independent, but sometimes all these decisions are difficult. Please guide me in making the right choices about what is best for me and my future. I pray you will also help me be a good example for my friends to help them avoid making harmful decisions.*

# THE QUESTION OF SEXUAL RELATIONSHIPS

Flee from sexual immorality. All other sins a person commits are outside the body, but whoever sins sexually sins against their own body. Do you not know that your bodies are temples of the Holy Spirit, who is in you, whom you have received from God? You are not your own; you were bought at a price. Therefore, honor God with your bodies.

**1 Corinthians 6:18–20**

Adolescence and young adulthood coincide with the awakening of sexual awareness. God created us to be sexual beings to continue to populate our planet. Sexual desire is a natural part of our humanity. Sexual urges aren't wrong or evil. It's how we respond that has the potential to create problems.

The Apostle Paul reminded the Church at Corinth the Holy Spirit resides within them (and us). We honor God when we stand strong against actions that abuse our bodies or cause harm to others. While an intimate relationship is a beautiful aspect of a loving marriage, sex before marriage can lead to unplanned pregnancies, dangerous diseases, and heartbreak.

Chances are you have faced these questions in high school: should I or shouldn't I have sex? No matter what your previous decisions were, the same questions will arise in college. More freedom provides more opportunities for intimate relationships. But again, no matter your previous experiences, each relationship brings a new opportunity for you to delay sexual activity—to honor your body and those with whom you are involved by protecting against the potential negative consequences of sex outside of marriage.

> *Prayer: Father, sometimes I think I'm so wise in the ways of the world, and at other times, I'm frightened by how little I know about life. Please guide us to make smart decisions about our intimate relationships.*

# Keep on Track

## Getting Lost on the Journey

Several years ago, my husband and I planned a visit to one of the smaller South Carolina beaches. The location was somewhat isolated and signage along the journey was poor. My cell phone service was spotty, and the GPS kept failing. We were soon hopelessly lost and argued about what to do.

He demanded I call our daughter (a smart move on his part, I admit). After explaining where we were (road numbers and landmarks), she could pull up a map on her phone and give us specific directions to get to our destination. My husband and I made it to our hotel, still on speaking terms.

In my career as a college professor, I've had students who get lost on their journey. When they reach out for help, I've assisted some of them in finding their way back to their pathway. Sadly, there are memories of other students who disappeared and left school before I even knew there was a problem.

When I first met John, I was impressed with his personality, energy, and attentiveness in class. He was outgoing and engaged enthusiastically in class discussions. One day, John didn't come to class. I emailed him but didn't receive a response. After several more absences and unanswered emails, I completed a student alert form to seek help in finding out what issues were keeping John from attending class. John never returned to class, and later, I received notification that he had withdrawn from school.

Several semesters later, John was again back in one of my classes. The same circumstances repeated. He was at first very much engaged and then stopped attending. I sought more information and learned that John had exhibited this pattern in numerous classes.

We don't always want to admit we have a problem, but the only way to seek help for a problem is to acknowledge we have one. Fortunately, John didn't get completely lost on the journey. After several incidences of stumbling off his pathway to graduation, he received counseling. With support from his family and more individual attention from the faculty, John completed his course of study and graduated.

John first believed he could solve his issues on his own. Even after withdrawing from school two previous times, John resisted talking with his advisor, teachers, and counselors at school. However, John did make the right decision to tell his parents. With their support, John finally accepted that he needed help—that this was not a problem he could solve on his own. With support and assistance from multiple areas, both on campus and from his family, John developed coping strategies and skills to allow him to achieve academically while meeting the mental and physical challenges which previously prevented his ability to complete his coursework.

John's case is not an isolated incident. Many students falter as mental, emotional, and academic challenges become overwhelming. It's important for students to watch for signs signaling the need to seek help.

Watch for:

- Academic struggles—unable to keep up with course requirements; not completing homework on time; poor grades on assignments and/or tests.
- Attendance problems—not attending class (every class, except when ill) can cause severe academic problems.
- Lack of interest—when students lose sight of their purpose (successfully completing college); emotional and academic support is needed.
- Mental, emotional, or physical issues that interfere with the student's ability to succeed in school.

Your college will have programs and personnel to assist you in your time of need. Please reach out for help when you are struggling. More information on how and when to seek assistance follows in this next section.

# CHOOSING THE RIGHT PATH

Whether you turn to the right or to the left, your ears will hear a voice behind you saying, "This is the way; walk in it."

**Isaiah 30:21**

The pathways in college are fraught with pitfalls, stumbling blocks, and temptations. At every turn, there are distractions to steer you off the road of success and force you into risky behaviors, sin, and failure.

Hopefully, your goals when coming to college are to succeed in completing your degree, prepare yourself for a career, and grow in wisdom and maturity. You may have other goals as well—being a successful student-athlete, preparing for graduate school, or going into business. The pathway you take to achieve these goals will determine whether you succeed.

How can you stay on the right path and not be blocked, stalled, or wrecked on the journey to complete your education?

- Keep your long-term goals in mind.
- Set achievable short-term goals that lead to a successful journey to meet your long-term goals.
- Maintain regular contact with your support system (family, mentors, academic advisor).

- Surround yourself with friends who have similar goals (completing college).
- Develop social relationships that support your academic plans.
- Avoid actions (risky behaviors) that cause detours from the pathway to achieve your goals.

*Prayer: Gracious Father, I pray my goals are in obedience to your will for my life. Help me develop a plan to achieve these goals and direct my path as I complete my college degree. Please grant me discernment and guide me in developing relationships that support my plans to be a successful college student. I pray you will provide mentors to support me on this journey.*

# Remember the Goal

So we fix our eyes not on what is seen, but on what is unseen, since what is seen is temporary, but what is unseen is eternal.

**2 Corinthians 4:18**

You've had goals all your life, and this new journey (college) is no exception. One of your goals is to do your best in school. Otherwise, you will waste your time and your parents' (or someone else's) money. The college/university experience should be enjoyable, but fun isn't the first priority.

When you throw a ball or run a race, it's important to keep your eye on the target—to know what the goal is, to have your focus on your plan for success. Goals are important at any stage of life. Some examples for a college student:

- Go to all classes each day (keep up with online classes).
- Don't procrastinate (stay ahead on assignments).
- Turn homework in on time.
- Get involved in campus life, but not to the extent it interferes with academics.
- Avoid alcohol and drugs.
- Make good grades.

These are just some examples; your list may vary. But, as the Apostle Paul writes, the unseen goals are of utmost importance. Graduation may seem far away for a freshman, but those four years pass quickly. Stay focused on the distant goals too.

Your most important task will be to maintain your relationship with your heavenly Father. Read your Bible. Join a faith-based campus group. Does your college have campus worship services? Can you travel home to church or find one near campus? Develop friendships that share your faith.

> *Prayer: My most important goal is to keep my eyes on you, my Father. I pray for guidance in all decisions and for your help in finding friends in my faith.*

# Be Aware of Danger from Within

> People will be lovers of themselves, lovers of money, boastful, proud, abusive, disobedient to their parents, ungrateful, unholy, without love, unforgiving, slanderous, without self-control, brutal, not lovers of the good, treacherous, rash, conceited, lovers of pleasure rather than lovers of God.
>
> **2 Timothy 3:2–4**

Your college or university campus will be a microcosm of society, displaying a variety of behaviors. You will meet students who are not interested in receiving an education but have come to campus only in the pursuit of pleasure (a good time). You will meet students without self-control or good judgment who will indulge in dangerous behaviors. There will be students in your classes unwilling to focus academically and will tempt you to ignore your studies.

It will require strength and courage for you to resist those who would distract you from your goal of doing well in school. Some helpful strategies:

- Choose friends that have similar interests and goals as you.
- Analyze every suggestion for an activity with the question: *Will this action positively or negatively*

*affect my ability to succeed in school and achieve my goals?*

- Avoid situations where you may be persuaded to participate in activities that can cause you or others harm.
- If something doesn't "feel right," get away from the situation.
- Remember that it takes courage to do the right thing.

*Prayer: Father, I'm excited to meet other students and form new friendships. Help me make wise decisions in choosing friends. Please help me to always consider how my actions may affect others and my future goals. I pray I can be a good example for others in making smart decisions.*

# RESPONDING TO TRIALS AND TROUBLES

For our light and momentary troubles are achieving for us an eternal glory that far outweighs them all.

**2 Corinthians 4:17**

There will be trials and troubles.

That's a scary thought. You're in your first semester of college, and I'm already warning you about trials and troubles. But you've experienced those before, haven't you?

These trials may vary somewhat from the ones you've had in previous schooling. You're more independent now and will be held responsible and accountable for your actions. Mom, Dad, family, and support may seem far away (even if you are in school in your hometown).

Confusion about an assignment, a traffic mishap, worry about failing a class, or a sudden illness won't seem like "light and momentary trouble." Worries and anxieties feel enormous when you're facing them alone, but don't let daily trials cause you to lose focus on your plan to do your best and reach your educational goals. Your long-term goal of successfully completing school, although a distant four years away, is your reward for the trials and troubles that come between now and graduation.

Even though you're on the road to independence, your parents or guardian will still assist you if needed.

Campus faculty and staff are also available when those trials and troubles threaten to derail you from your goal. Sometimes, you only need someone to listen. At other times, you may need advice. And, perhaps on rare occasions, you'll need an attitude adjustment or a firm dose of chastisement to "**settle down and get to work!**"

*Prayer: Father, when the trials and troubles come, help me know who to turn to for advice or for an "attitude adjustment." I'm striving to gain my independence, but sometimes, I'll probably need help and guidance to stay on track. Help me know when to ask for help.*

# TRIALS WE LEAST EXPECT—BIG ONES!

I will say of the Lord, "He is my refuge and my fortress, my God in whom I trust. Surely he will save you from the fowler's snare and from deadly pestilence."

**Psalm 91:2–3**

Spring 2020 will hold a long-lasting memory for everyone on Earth. The coronavirus developed in China during the winter of 2019 and, by spring, had spread throughout the world. Millions developed the disease and millions died as the pandemic continued.

The unthinkable happened—a world pandemic.

Students who experienced this trauma will not soon forget. School schedules were completely disrupted and online learning became the norm. Students, parents, and teachers struggled with adapting to new and unchartered territory. Athletes experienced the loss of their spring season. Proms, concerts, and graduation—special events students look forward to for a lifetime were canceled.

But as we watched and listened, people came together, finding new and alternative methods to accomplish important goals. We found new ways to utilize social media and technology to form community as COVID-19 forced isolation. We learned to appreciate and value our medical and service personnel who worked tirelessly to care for the sick and elderly.

We are still absorbing lessons learned from this crisis, but you will be carrying these experiences with you as you face a changing future—a "new normal." Always remember that God loves you. We are stronger together, and loving one another helps us through every crisis.

> *Prayer: Father, we still do not understand why this deadly virus ravaged us and changed our world so drastically. Help us remember to turn to you in times of crisis. We know trials will come, and some of those will seem too hard to bear. Help us trust in your care.*

## SUFFERING BUILDS CHARACTER?

Through whom we have gained access by faith into this grace in which we now stand. And we boast in the hope of the glory of God. Not only so, but we also glory in our sufferings, because we know that suffering produces perseverance, perseverance produces character, and character, hope. And hope does not put us to shame, because God's love has been poured out into our hearts through the Holy Spirit, who has been given to us.

**Romans 5:2–5**

Does suffering build character?

Ouch—who wants to build character that way?

Admit it though, if things come too easy, we don't appreciate them as much. Think back to some of your happiest moments. Weren't many of those joyful experiences when you accomplished a challenging goal? Completing a difficult task—winning a prestigious award, achieving a personal best as an athlete? Your list of successful achievements is likely a long one as you enter college. A task that takes a lot of effort and hard work seems a more worthy goal and we receive more satisfaction when we achieve that tough challenge.

Trials make us stronger because we have to be strong to survive them. Trials make us wiser, too—if we learn from them.

So, remember . . .

When the hard times come (and they will) keep these things in mind:

- God is with you on this journey. He is only a prayer away.
- Those hard lessons you learn will make you stronger and wiser.
- Persevere (keep going) through those hard times.
- Suffering and persevering give us strength, character, and hope.
- God is loving, merciful, and full of grace, and we are the blessed recipients.

*Prayer: Father, I know there will be trials and suffering. I just pray that you will be with me and with the other students here. You've promised that you will not give us more burdens than we can bear, and I know you are with us. My hope is in you.*

# When You Want to Give Up

## "I CAN'T DO THIS—
## I'M GOING TO QUIT!"

She could hardly understand what her student was saying over the phone. "Wait, slow down . . . breathe," the teacher urged.

The student teacher sobbed as her mentor waited. When the sobs eased, the teacher requested, "Tell me what is wrong."

Between renewed bouts of tears and cries of "I can't do this!" the professor continued with patient waiting and listening. Finally, the problem emerged . . . middle school.

I've often told my students that the teachers I have the greatest admiration for teach preschool, kindergarten, and middle school. They ask why. "Because the students act the same," I respond.

"What do you mean?" my students query further.

"Middle school students have bigger bodies, but their behavior is a lot like kindergarteners, so it makes it extra hard to have good classroom management, deal with raging hormones, and accomplish productive learning." Sometimes I've even told my college students they fit in those categories, too (big bodies, childish behavior). But, that's a story for another time.

My student was challenged by her experience with middle school students—their disruptive behavior, their lack of cooperation, and their complete disregard for her instructional plans. In other words, they were being typical middle school students.

However, my first concern now was helping her find calm. I followed with a consult with her cooperating teacher at the middle school, and the three of us devised a plan to help our student achieve success in her student teaching.

Even in her emotional state, my student followed the correct procedure. Once she realized there was a problem, she approached it correctly by reaching out to me to let me know. (I'm not talking about the "I'm quitting" statement here—that was her emotions— but she let me know early on there was a problem). She informed me and asked for my help. Working together with her teacher at the middle school, we implemented strategies, offered ongoing mentoring, and continued to monitor and encourage her. My student successfully completed her student teaching. She took responsibility for her actions and reached out to me so I could do my job in helping her meet the challenge.

Remember, ask for help when the trials become too difficult.

# ASK FOR HELP

*Listen to my words, Lord, consider my lament. Hear my cry for help, my King and my God, for to you I pray.*

**Psalm 5:1–2**

No matter how well you are prepared for college, there will come a time you need help. It may be academic, social, emotional, physical, or some other issue. As always, God is just a prayer away. Cry out to him in your time of need. Sometimes just speaking of the issue (to God) will help you work out the problem. At other times, you will need to step out further and seek other guidance.

In advance, you should know how to contact your professors if you need to ask questions, request clarification or assistance on an assignment, or report an issue of concern (illness, family emergency, etc.) Your instructor will likely provide his/her contact information on the class syllabus. Students should be proactive in approaching a professor for help. Ask for assistance *before* the assignment is due. If you know you are going to miss class due to a family emergency or other extenuating circumstances, email your professor **in advance** of the absence.

There are times when all students need extra support. Your college or university will have multiple programs and personnel to assist students with academic needs. It is a wise decision to investigate these programs during the early part of your first semester.

> *Prayer: Father God, I'm so thankful you are always just a prayer away. I know you hear me when I call to you for help. There may be times when I need to reach out to others for assistance. I pray you will guide me to know when those times come and give me the courage to seek help.*

# ASK FOR HELP
# (EVEN WHEN IT'S HARD)

But you, Lord, are a shield around me, my glory, the One who lifts my head high. I call out to the Lord, and he answers me from his holy mountain. I lie down and sleep; I wake again, because the Lord sustains me.

**Psalm 3:3–5**

It's hard to ask for help. It's scary to admit we don't understand and downright frightening to talk to a professor about a poor grade on a test or paper.

But what about those non-academic problems? (And yes, those will occur in college too.) There will be days when everything seems to go wrong—days when you are far behind in your schoolwork, days when you want to hide in a corner and pretend that school isn't important.

We all experience fear of the future—those what ifs. What if I fail this test? What if I don't pass this course? What if I can't be successful in college? What if I let down my team? What if no one likes me?

No matter how confident we are most of the time, sometimes we doubt our ability to succeed. We're afraid of failure and disappointing our family. Darkness creeps in, and we just want to give up.

That's when we most need to turn to God. Pour out our fears. Dwell with him in quietness and absorb his reassurance. There may also be times when we need to seek help from family or a counselor at school. It isn't a weakness to ask for help; it takes much more courage to seek help than it does to give up.

> *Prayer: Father, sometimes it's just too much. I want to give up. But, you Lord, are my shield. Please help me through those dark times and show me the path back to the light.*

# WHEN YOU MESS UP

For we do not have a high priest who is unable to empathize with our weaknesses, but we have one who has been tempted in every way, just as we are—yet he did not sin. Let us then approach God's throne of grace with confidence, so that we may receive mercy and find grace to help us in our time of need.

**Hebrews 4:15–16**

It will happen. You will mess up . . .

What to do?

An important part of working toward and gaining independence is owning your mistakes. It's inevitable (like taxes) that you sometimes fall short. Don't try to hide it or pretend mistakes didn't happen.

I'm not saying you blurt out every error you make, but I encourage you to face up to mistakes that have the potential to rob you of your goals. It's also important to admit and attempt to rectify actions that may cause harm to others.

Mistakes that can cause academic problems for you:

- Not completing an assignment.
- Not turning in assignments on time.
- Turning in poorly completed work.
- Missing class.
- Unprepared for tests or exams.

These are mistakes you will be held accountable for. Admit your errors to your instructor. Ask if you may redo a poorly done assignment for partial credit. Ask (in advance of due dates) for an appointment if there are aspects of an assignment you don't understand.

> *Prayer: Father, I pray you will help me be a conscientious student, that I attend all classes, do my work correctly and on time, and that I'm always prepared for tests. But when I don't—because we all mess up sometimes— help me admit my mistakes and do better.*

# WHEN DISASTER STRIKES

Have mercy on me, my God, for in you I take refuge. I will take refuge in the shadow of your wings until the disaster has passed.

**Psalm 57:1**

Many people are praying for you—for protection and safety as you complete your education. But sometimes, a crisis may occur.

- You might fail a test.
- Perhaps you forget to complete an important assignment.
- Or you completed an assignment incorrectly because you didn't follow directions.
- You may miss a class because you overslept.
- You could be involved in an accident or become ill.

Missing classes is not a good thing. Most instructors plan each class carefully, providing important information and activities to facilitate learning. Information from each class prepares a foundation for the material taught in future classes. Strive to attend every class except in case of illness. Too many absences can lead to failure. Even a single absence can cause you to miss important content that will affect overall learning and test performance.

Your professors have high expectations for you and expect you to be accountable for your attendance and performance in class. But they are not out to get you. **Your professors want you to succeed**. If you are struggling in a class, make an appointment with your professor to get their recommendations as to how you can improve your performance.

Remember, there is help available on campus if you need tutoring, writing assistance, or strategies to improve your study skills. Be proactive (don't procrastinate) in seeking assistance.

*Prayer: Father, I pray for your mercy and protection from disaster, not only for me but for all students here. Guide us to seek assistance when needed and not allow our pride to prevent us from making wise decisions. Please be with our faculty and staff as well.*

# WHEN YOU ARE SICK

Heal me, Lord and I will be healed; save me and I will be
saved, for you are the one I praise.

**Jeremiah 17:14**

When groups of people live in close contact with each
other, there are more illnesses to share; more opportunities to be sick. At some point during the year, you will
likely develop colds, flu, or other contagious illnesses.
Though we hope and pray a COVID-19 (or other diseases) pandemic will not strike again, history informs us
that diseases spread among humans.

Practice good hygiene to eliminate your exposure to
illnesses. Good hand washing is still the best protection
to prevent illnesses from spreading. Keep your immune
system strong with healthy nutrition and adequate rest
(see the wellness section for more information about
maintaining healthy habits).

If you are sick and need to be absent, let your instructors know (in advance, if possible). Let your teachers
know, by email, the status of your illness, and keep them
up to date if you need to miss more than one class. As soon
as your health allows, be back in touch to follow up on
notes missed and assignments to complete. Some professors may require a note from the Student Health Center or
your doctor before allowing you to make up missed work.

Although you won't tell your parents or guardians everything that goes on at college, you need to let them know when you are sick. Some illnesses can be very serious and need medical care. Always let someone know if you are sick so they can regularly check on you.

*Prayer: Father, the thought of becoming sick when my parents aren't around to take care of me is scary. I pray you will be with us—all the students here—to keep us healthy. If we do get sick, help us know where to go for help.*

# WHEN YOUR SOUL IS WEARY

My soul is weary with sorrow; strengthen me according to
your word.

**Psalm 119:28**

Some days you will be so tired, weak, and sad that you
want to forget all about college, get in your car, and
go home.

"I've had enough! I quit!"

We all have times when we are overwhelmed with
life. We just want to crawl into our beds, cover up, and
wait until it—whatever stumbling block that has interfered—is over. As a college student, these trials will
seem as tall and insurmountable as Mt. Everest.

You may feel lost and alone, not knowing who to turn
to for help. Sometimes we want to cry out to God as did
the Psalmist, **"Why, Lord, do you stand so far off? Why
do you hide yourself in times of trouble? (Psalm 10:1)**

Thankfully, we can cry out our doubt and anxiety to our
Lord Jesus. He always listens. He will carry our burdens.

Come to me, all you who are weary and burdened, and I will
give you rest. Take my yoke upon you and learn from me,
for I am gentle and humble in heart and you will find rest
for your souls. For my yoke is easy and my burden is light.

**Matthew 11:28–20**

Take your burdens to Jesus through prayer. He will lighten your load. Ask Him for guidance about where to seek help.

> *Prayer: Jesus, I feel so weary and burdened. I don't know what to do. Your word tells me you will ease my burden and my soul will find rest in you. Thank you, Lord Jesus. Please guide me in strengthening my faith and seeking the earthly help I need to get through this trial.*

## EACH DAY IS A NEW DAY

Let the morning bring me word of your unfailing love, for I
have put my trust in you. Show me the way I should go, for
to you I entrust my life.

**Psalm 143:8**

Some days it will seem nothing goes right and everything bad that could possibly happen does.

- You overslept.
- You forgot an assignment.
- You bombed a test.
- You had an argument with your roommate.
- Your boyfriend/girlfriend is mad at you.
- The food in the cafeteria is terrible.
- You're coming down with a cold and feeling rotten.

The list of stuff that can go wrong is endless. The
only sure thing is bad situations will happen.

There will be days you wish you had stayed in bed.
You may want to crawl under a rock and hide; retreat to
your room and close the door or get in your car, drive
home, and never come back.

But, in these circumstances, it's your reaction that
makes the difference. What did you learn? Can you
avoid the same mistake in the future? Can you try again?

Remember, God is with you. His love is unfailing. You can trust Him with your fears, hopes, and dreams. He is only a prayer away. When those terrible days surround you and steal away your self-confidence, pour out your frustration to Him. Ask for His guidance and the strength to go forward to another day. He will give you the courage to persevere through those hard days.

Tomorrow is a new day!

*Prayer: Father, I know I will have challenges, but it's hard when everything goes wrong. Help me learn from every situation, especially when I mess up and make mistakes. Help me keep trying.*

# GOD IS ALWAYS FAITHFUL

Let us hold unswervingly to the hope we profess, for he
who promised is faithful.

**Hebrews 10:23**

There will be times of doubt. You may ask yourselves
questions such as,

- Am I at the right school?
- Am I in the right major?
- Should I join this organization?
- Should I seek academic help such as tutoring or
  writing skills?
- Should I end my relationship with this person or
  group because they are interfering with my ability
  to achieve my goal of completing my education?

Or perhaps the most frightening . . .

**Should I give up—go home—and never come
back to this school?**

Major decisions are tough—especially if we're trying
to make them on our own. You may, at some point, feel
overwhelmed and not know to whom to turn for help.

Remember, God is faithful. He wants the best for
you. He wants you to succeed in your goal to finish your
degree. When those times of doubt creep in (and they

will)—**PRAY.** Sometimes a place of quiet solitude and reflection will bring peace. At other times of self-questioning, you may want to seek out your campus pastor, a former teacher, a family member, or a faithful friend. In your conversation, be open about your doubts and fears. Ask for prayer. If they share advice or wisdom, listen, but remember, the decision is yours to make. Be sure to consider your long-term goals as you make short-term changes.

> *Prayer: Father, I know you are always faithful. You will not leave me alone when I am afraid or worried. Please guide me in all my decisions, especially when I'm having doubts about my path and ability to succeed. Please show me the way.*

# Wellness

## "I Didn't Think I Could Do It!"

The warmth on our shoulders was just right—not too hot for hiking—as a gentle breeze flowed across the mountain. Students chatted in pairs or small groups as they trekked up the steep slope, taking frequent breaks to rest or peruse the countryside.

Ireland is lovely.

Even lovelier, from my perspective, was viewing this wonderful country with a group of student education majors and colleagues whose company I greatly enjoyed.

For most of our time in Ireland, we toured schools, talked with students and educators about their experiences, and compared ideas of innovations to encourage the love of learning. It must be a universal concern; teachers everywhere want to provide their students with the best educational experience possible. And even with an ocean between us, teachers from both countries recognized our mutual worries about our students' lack of motivation.

Today, however, we put worries aside as we traversed a steep slope with the promise of a beautiful view from the summit.

My colleague and I were at the rear of the group, making sure none of our charges became lost on the journey. He was in his forties and I in my fifties—both living active lifestyles—were undaunted by the climb. It would have been another story if we were jogging up the mountain, but our pace was moderate.

Less than halfway, we encountered one of our students, already overwhelmed with the physical challenge of the climb. Her face red and sweaty, she gasped, "I can't do this."

We stopped and waited until she was able to breathe somewhat normally. "Are you okay?"

"I can't climb this mountain." A tear mingled with the sweat trickling down her face. "It's too hard." She swiped at her face as she choked back a sob with a hiccup.

My colleague and I stared at each other. Silently, we agreed on what we needed to do.

"Sit here a little while," he encouraged her. There was a bench nearby.

"It's a little warm today," I commented. "We need to be careful not to try to climb too quickly."

"I'm in terrible shape," she moaned. "I'll never make it. You two go on, and I'll just wait here."

"We'll wait a little while with you," my colleague said. We chatted about unrelated things.

After she rested a few minutes and appeared to be breathing more normally, I asked, "Want to go a little further? There are benches along the way where we can rest."

She looked up the hill, then at each of us. "You really can go on. I'll be okay here, and I'll walk back down when the others come."

"We'll just stay with you then," I responded.

"You're not going to give up, are you?" she asked us.

"No," my co-worker and I said at the same time, and we all laughed. It brightened the sunshine to see a smile replace her tears.

"Okay, I'll go a little further."

My colleague reminded her. "The benches are for people to rest. When you need to stop, just let us know. We'll go slow."

A glimmer of hope crossed her face. "Do you really think I can make it?"

"Yes!" we both said, and we all laughed again.

So . . . slowly, we made the trip, resting whenever she needed to. The view at the top was worth the long journey. And the joy on her face for her success gifted us an even greater reward. "I didn't think I could do it, but I did!" She thanked us profusely as she kept saying, "I couldn't have done it without you."

There were many wonderful memories of our trip to Ireland, but her joy at achieving a goal she thought beyond her was one of the best.

Our student emailed both of us after our return to the U.S. She thanked us again but also expressed the desire to exercise to improve her physical condition. She recognized the two of us, even though much older, were in much better physical health than she was. She also realized it was within her power to do something about it. She could change her daily habits to strengthen and improve her physical health.

She requested some recommendations, which I shared with her. She wanted to improve her overall health and well-being.

Our health and well-being are, for the most part, under *our* control. The choices we make (how active we are, what we eat, self-care) are primarily our decisions. This section called Wellness offers guidance to help you maintain a healthier lifestyle.

# YOU ARE WONDERFULLY MADE

For you created my inmost being; you knit me together in my mother's womb. I praise you because I am fearfully and wonderfully made; your works are wonderful; I know that full well.

**Psalm 139:13–14**

When we think about the human body, we recognize that we truly are "fearfully and wonderfully made." It's so amazing that we can see, hear, smell, taste, touch, move, think, reason, speak, love and so much more. According to the Bible, we are God's most treasured creation.

The Book of Genesis describes God's Creation. Each day represents an aspect of God's work. The author ends the description of each day's events with the affirmation that "God saw it was good." On the sixth day:

God created mankind in his own image, in the image of God he created them; male and female he created them.

**Genesis 1:27**

Following this,

God saw all he had made and it was very good.

**Genesis 1:31**

When God created the world, it was good. When God made humans, it was *very* good. We are God's special creation.

So . . . when you are away from home, how do you care for this awesome creation (your body) God has gifted to you? In this next section of devotions, we focus on some wellness habits that will keep your body healthy, while you honor God by taking care of His creation—YOU!

> *Prayer: Father, I praise you for your awesome power and glory. I know I am special because you made me as part of your creation. Please guide me to make decisions to honor you and keep my body healthy and able to work for you.*

# FEEDING THE TEMPLE

Then God said, "I give you every seed-bearing plant on the face of the whole earth and every tree that has fruit with seed in it. They will be yours for food."

**Genesis1:29**

First Corinthians 6:19 tells us that our bodies are temples of the Holy Spirit. What do you feed your temple?

What are your favorite foods? Are you already missing home cooking?

Food in the college cafeteria or other on-campus eateries probably won't taste like your mother or father's cooking. Your inclination (and that of your friends) will probably be to eat out—a lot. Fast food is typically loaded with fat, sugar, and calories, all of which make food taste good, but is very unhealthy (and expensive). If you're not careful, you'll pack on the legendary "freshman fifteen" or more.

So . . . how to survive campus food or eating out without packing on the pounds?

- Eliminate how often you eat out—it's costly and difficult to select healthy choices in a restaurant.
- As much as possible, avoid fried foods—frying adds calories and reduces the healthful benefit of any food.

- In the cafeteria, try to make healthy choices— lean meat (such as chicken or fish), fresh vegetables and fruits, skim milk, whole grains, smaller portions of desserts, and low-calorie snack foods.
- Limit consumption of pizza, hotdogs, hamburgers, sodas, and other types of "fast food." These foods are loaded with fat and calories. Alcoholic beverages are also high in calories.
- Drink more water!
- Eat more fresh fruits and vegetables (see next devotion for more information).

*Prayer: Father, I miss being home, my favorite foods and restaurants I like best, but I'm trying to adjust. Please help me along the way and guide me to make healthier choices in what I eat and drink.*

# FIVE A DAY!

"Please test your servants for ten days: Give us nothing but vegetables to eat and water to drink." At the end of ten days they looked healthier and better nourished than any of the young men who ate the royal food.

**Daniel 1:12,15**

God had a great plan when he recommended fruits and vegetables (Genesis 1:29). They are packed with complex carbohydrates, vitamins, minerals, and fiber (good stuff) and are filling (helps us not to eat so much of the bad stuff). Fruits and vegetables are loaded with antioxidants, which strengthen our immune system (important to keep us from getting sick).

Try to make fruits and vegetables prepared in a healthy way, a regular part of your diet (sorry, French fries aren't healthy because they are fried). Healthy preparation means choosing fresh whenever possible while limiting additions of fat and sugar. If vegetables are cooked, be careful of additives such as salt, butter, and sauces. Most Americans (including young people) consume dangerously high amounts of sodium that cause negative health issues. Salads are good choices, but select dressings that are lower in fat, sugar, and sodium. Fresh fruits are a good choice to replace a high-calorie dessert.

Aim for *five* or more servings of fruits and vegetables each day that are prepared in a healthy way. A serving is a medium-sized piece of fresh fruit, a half cup of cooked vegetables or fruit, and a generous portion of raw leafy greens for a salad. Eating a salad every day, topped with a variety of additional fruits and vegetables and vinegar-based dressing, is a good choice.

*Prayer: Father, some of these fruits and vegetables are not my idea of good food, but I pray you'll guide me to try new healthy foods.*

## Be Physically Active

Dear friend, I pray that you may enjoy good health and
that all may go well with you, even as your soul is getting
along well.

**3 John 1:2**

Regular physical exercise maintains health-related fitness and provides great benefits to your overall health:

- Strengthens the heart muscle, other muscles, and bones.
- Reduces the likelihood of developing heart disease or diabetes.
- Reduces the risk of some cancers.
- Helps maintain a healthy weight.
- Improves alertness and mental health.
- Strengthens the immune system.
- Helps us cope with stress.
- Reduces risks of osteoporosis.
- Promotes longer and better quality of life.

To achieve health-related fitness, you should exercise at least three to five times per week for thirty to sixty minutes each day. Your activity plan should include both aerobic exercise (walking, jogging, dancing, aerobics, swimming, etc.) and resistance exercises (weight lifting, push-ups, crunches, planks, etc.). For those with time constraints, the recommended thirty to sixty minutes per day can be divided into smaller increments throughout the day.

As a college student, you will have on-campus opportunities for exercise, such as a fitness center; exercise, dance, or aerobic classes; activity classes for college credit and areas to walk and jog. Walking to classes instead of driving adds activity time. If you are a commuter, parking further away from your destination provides walking time. Using stairs instead of elevators adds additional exercise.

Being physically active provides many benefits for the short-term (good health now) and the long-term (healthy for a lifetime). Taking good care of yourself is an important part of your college journey.

*Prayer: Father, I know exercise is important for my health, but often I don't have time or motivation. Help me be active for better health.*

# BE HOLY AND PLEASING TO GOD

Therefore, I urge you, brothers and sisters, in view of God's mercy, to offer your bodies as a living sacrifice, holy and pleasing to God—this is your true and proper worship.

**Romans 12:1**

We've talked about temptations—behaviors that will seem enticing and harmless but could cause you to lose sight of your goals.

In the above Scripture, the Apostle Paul reminds the Romans (and us) that our God is merciful and loving. In response, Paul urges us to offer our bodies as a *living* sacrifice, to be holy and pleasing to our Lord.

How can our bodies be holy and pleasing to God?

We can keep our bodies (this amazing creation) healthy so that we honor and please God:

- Eat a nutritious diet, emphasizing lean protein, low fats, healthy carbohydrates, and lots of fruits and vegetables.
- Exercise regularly with a fitness plan appropriate for your needs.
- Get adequate sleep (which for a college student means being well organized and avoiding procrastination so that you avoid all-nighters for last-minute cramming).

- Drive safely (within speed limits, wear seat belts, and no road rage).
- Avoid alcohol, tobacco, and other drugs.
- Abstain from sexual activity that could lead to STIs (sexually transmitted infections) or unplanned pregnancies.

By taking care of our bodies, we can honor God by showing appreciation for the marvelous gift of life and health. We can also better serve Him when we are healthy.

> *Prayer: I want to be holy and pleasing to you, Father, but it's hard to do all the things I need to keep my body healthy. Please help me do my best to honor you in all things and show me the ways that I can best serve you.*

# Do Good

## CALLED TO SERVE

**"M**a'am? I'm sorry to keep you when I know you might have other duties to take care of."

I looked up from gathering my materials to return to the office. The young man before me held a cap in his hands, twisting it around in his hands.

"It's fine, Wayne. What do you need?"

His dark eyes sparkled. "I wanted to talk to you about our service project." He stuffed the hat into his back pocket, leaving his hands free to gesture as he spoke. "I have an idea."

We had just reviewed the syllabus where I briefly described the service component for the class. I was amazed and impressed that he already had an idea. In many of my classes, I required service projects, reflecting my belief that we share our love with others through the gift of our time. This assignment isn't always greeted with enthusiasm by my students.

Placing my books back on the desk, I gestured to one of the tables just vacated by the rapidly departing students. "Got time to tell me about it?"

A smile as bright as the September sunshine outside the window transformed his face as we both sat.

"My dad is a veteran, and he has friends that are veterans. Many of them were wounded in service and are on disability now." He glanced down at the table. "Actually, I need to go further back. My grandfather is a Vietnam vet and was sprayed by Agent Orange. He has cancer now."

"I'm so sorry. That's hard for all of you."

He met my gaze. Moisture glistened in his eyes. "He wants to do something to help before he dies." He looked down again and swallowed.

"And you want to help him?"

"Yes." He met my gaze as his eyes lit with anticipation.

"Do you already have a plan?"

That big smile again brought sunshine into the room. "Grandpa has a farm and a pond. We want to clear a path to the pond and make it accessible for those in wheelchairs so they can get to the pond and duck hunt."

I sat back in my chair in surprise. This would be a tremendous project—a *lot* of work. Depending on the amount of clearing, heavy equipment might be needed. Ramps, built to code, would be necessary. Safety protocols must be followed. Liability issues would need addressing. This project would not only be time-consuming (much more than the ten hours required for the class, but costly). I didn't immediately respond.

His smile dimmed as he noted my expression. "You don't think it's a good idea?"

"I think it is a great idea, but it's going to be expensive and need lots of hours of labor." I shook my head.

A tentative smile returned. "I've got that all worked out. My grandpa is going to pay for everything. We've already contacted the Wounded Warrior Program, and they are supportive. You know about Wounded Warriors?"

I nodded, and he enthusiastically continued. I've got friends that have already agreed to help and our neighbors want to help too." He hesitated a moment. "What do you think?"

My heart swelled with pride in this caring young man. I wanted to sing with joy at his earnest enthusiasm. He and his family saw a need and were developing a plan to meet it.

Now my smile shared some sunshine too. "I think it's a wonderful idea. I think some of your classmates might want to volunteer too."

*I don't know what your destiny will be,*
*but one thing I know: the only ones among you*
*who will be really happy are those who*
*have sought and found how to serve.*
Albert Schweitzer

# PURSUE RIGHTEOUSNESS

He who pursues righteousness and love finds life,
prosperity, and honor.

**Proverbs 21:21**

We've previously discussed avoiding negative temptations that come your way with the increased independence that college brings. Sometimes that's easier said than done. While some actions are clear dangers, others may be less easy to recognize as potentially destructive. One way to help you avoid harmful behaviors is to focus on being righteous.

***Righteous*** is an adjective that describes behavior. The Encarta Dictionary provides several definitions:

- Observing strict morality—always behaving according to a religious or moral code.
- Justifiable—behavior considered to be correct or justified.
- Responding to injustice—recognizing when actions are not justified and responding appropriately.

Using these guidelines to determine your actions can help you avoid behaviors that are harmful. You do not want to participate in activities that may interfere with your ability to complete your college degree. Nor do you want to cause the failure of other students. Always remember that God is just a prayer away to help you discern if a particular action is righteous.

Another way of filtering our actions is to use the "Golden Rule" many of us learned as children: "*Do unto others as you would have them do unto you.*" We should always consider our deeds through the lens of how our behavior can benefit or harm others. Actions that cause others to suffer, bring shame or hardship to you or other students, or interfere with your or others' ability to complete their educational goals should be avoided.

> *Prayer: Father, please help us be supportive of each other. Please grant us wisdom to make responsible decisions so we do no harm to ourselves or others. Help us demonstrate integrity and honor. I pray I may be a good example to others.*

# SERVE OTHERS

> For we are God's handiwork, created in Christ Jesus to do good works, which God prepared in advance for us to do.
>
> **Ephesians 2:10**

Perhaps you have already been active in a life of service to others through your church, mission trips, high school experiences, or within your community. If so, thank you for reaching out to give love to God's children.

On the other hand, you may not have had experience in being a servant to others. College is a wonderful environment to either begin or continue a life of service.

Many of your classes may require a community service component. I hope you will embrace this opportunity and find it rewarding, rather than considering service as just a task to complete. Many clubs, sororities, fraternities, or athletic teams actively engage in activities to help others.

Jesus provided the example of service,

> "And whoever wants to be first must be your slave—just as the Son of Man did not come to be served, but to serve, and to give his life as a ransom for many."
>
> **Matthew 20:27–28**

This doesn't mean that we are required to sacrifice our life, but by giving of our time in service to others, we are giving of ourselves.

It can be a challenge to find time in your schedule for service, but the rewards are bountiful. The joy in the eyes and hearts of those you assist is priceless. Your visit may be the brightest part of their day. And, in the giving, you are bountifully blessed in return.

> *Prayer: As your children, Lord, we are called to serve you. Sometimes volunteering makes me uncomfortable. Please help me recognize we are all your children and guide me in service to you as I help others.*

## CARING FOR OTHERS

Do nothing out of selfish ambition or vain conceit. Rather in humility value others above yourselves, not looking to your own interests, but each of you to the interest of others.

**Philippians 2:3**

Humans are born egocentric. For a baby, his or her needs (food, sleep, warmth, kindness, safety, and a clean diaper) are the most important. The newborn has no concept of patience, sharing, giving, or putting the needs of others in front of their own desires. Babies are born selfish so they can let caregivers know when they are in need.

But, as we grow and mature, we should develop the ability to care for others. Your parents, guardians, extended family, teachers, and other mentors have likely worked with you to develop **altruism**, *an attitude or way of behaving marked by unselfish concern for the welfare of others.*[5]

There will be many opportunities in college to demonstrate altruism. Some of your classes will probably require service learning, hours spent devoted to helping others. There are many locations on campus and in your community for you to serve others.

I urge you to embrace these opportunities, rather than viewing them as a burden. At the time, you may be over-

---

5    *Encarta World English Dictionary* (1999), Anne Soukhanov, editor. St. Martin›s Press, s.v. "altruism (n.)."

whelmed by many assignments and claims on your time. But the reward you receive by helping others will go far beyond just completing a requirement or earning points for participation.

Sometimes, the most loving and powerful gift we can give to others is our time.

> *Prayer: Father, I realize I'm going to be overwhelmed by all I need to do. In fact, I'm already feeling some worry about getting it all done. But I pray you will guide me to the place you believe I should be to help others in need.*

# A FUTURE GENERATION

Let this be written for a future generation, that a people not yet created may praise the Lord.

**Psalm 102:10**

You are our future.

That's probably a scary thought for you. You've just experienced the many challenges of high school. Now you're facing the bigger mountain of college. And, looming beyond that peak, is the rocky and far-reaching mountain range of life.

As I write this particular devotion, it is June 6. This morning on television, I watched some of the ceremony commemorating the Anniversary of D-Day, the Allied invasion of Normandy, which marked the beginning of the end of World War II in Europe. Thousands of brave young soldiers died on the beaches of Normandy on June 6, 1944. Many of them still teenagers. Those brave, young men and women who gave their lives in World War II were our future. They died so a people not yet born (everyone born since 1944) might have life and breath to praise the Lord, serve Him, and live with the blessings of freedom.

We all have an obligation to give to the future by doing our best in the present. Just as you and I have benefitted from the hard work and sacrifice of those who came before, all who come after you will reap the harvest of your contributions.

> *Prayer: Father, the future is unknown, and that makes it scary sometimes. But I know you promised to be with me always. I pray you will help me honor those who had a part in getting me to this place in my life—my parents, grandparents, other family, teachers, and all who contributed to the foundation and preservation of our country. And please, help me do my best in school.*

# RUN YOUR RACE
# WITH PERSEVERANCE

Therefore, since we are surrounded by such a great cloud of witnesses, let us throw off everything that hinders and the sin that so easily entangles. And let us run with perseverance the race marked out for us, fixing our eyes on Jesus, the pioneer and perfecter of faith. For the joy set before him he endured the cross, scorning its shame and sat down at the right hand of the throne of God.

**Hebrews 12:1–2**

Each of us has our journey. God's plans for you are unique. You are like no other, and that frees you to make decisions that are best for you. God has a pathway, a race, marked out just for you.

Being an athlete requires training, self-discipline, determination, and a strong desire to be one's best. Your journey as a successful college student requires those same attributes. There will be days when you are exhausted, tired, and weary as you struggle to see the finish line of your "race" to complete your degree.

But you can do it! It takes one task at a time—one day at a time; one semester at a time; one year at a time—and you will achieve your goal of completing your college degree. There may be times you need to refer to sections in this devotional to give yourself advice and encouragement. Even after you complete your first year, there will still be situations when you need to ask for help. Remember, seeking help in times of trial is a sign of strength, taking ownership of whatever the problem might be.

*Prayer: Father, together, we have made many steps in this first-year journey. Thank you. I pray you will continue to be with me.*

# Stay the Course

## WHEN STUBBORNNESS IS GOOD

Number 23.

Wendy stared down at the basketball jersey as she folded the clean uniform to return to the coach. The royal blue silk fabric is still as smooth to the touch as at the beginning of the season. No nicks or tears needed repair before returning. Warming the bench didn't cause much wear and tear on a uniform, except maybe to shine the seat.

A year of sitting on the bench—working hard during practice, hustling every moment to help the first-string players get better. But no time in a game—not a single minute—no matter if the team won or lost or the range of score, #23 never entered a game.

She ran her fingers over the bold gold lettering of her school and number. She didn't feel so bold now. The start of a season is filled with hope, but discouragement settles like a heavy blanket when hard work brings no fulfillment or satisfaction.

*I want to quit.* A junior year, filled with hard work—wasted.

She finished folding the uniform and placed it with her schoolbooks.

### Three months later

"You had a called from Emily," Mom said.

Wendy looked up from her chore of shelling peas. "What? When did she call?"

"She's the captain of the basketball team, isn't she? She phoned while you were in the garden."

"Yes," she mumbled, her hands momentarily stilled at the news. She grabbed another pod to shell. "Did she say what she wanted?"

"Some of the team are going to get together for pick-up basketball this summer. She's hoping you will come."

Hands working automatically on the thick pods of peas, her brain raced. *You should have told them all last year you were quitting.*

But she hadn't told them—she'd not talked with anyone about the despair and discouragement of working so hard for nothing.

"You want to go?" Mom asked. "I think she said Tuesday nights. You can call her back to check."

*No, I don't want to go.* She kept that answer to herself as her mind went back to last season. *But, neither do I want to be a quitter.*

"I guess I will. I'll give her a call." Stubbornness, she inherited from both sides of the family. Only time would tell if it would prove to be helpful.

### *Senior year*

As it turned out, being stubborn and determined can prove beneficial. Number 23 played in every game. Her tenacity, hustle, and refusal to give up earned her a position in the starting line-up and being chosen as first-team All-Conference.

Years later, Wendy pondered the reasons the coach never put her into a game during her junior year season. As a sophomore, Wendy had been an occasional substitute, not seeing a lot of playing time, but enough to look forward to her junior year with high expectations. Those high hopes were dashed with the advent of a new coach, just out of college. The new coach, an outstanding player when in school, had no experience as a coach. Wendy suspected Coach didn't even realize Wendy never entered a game during the season.

Wendy acknowledged to herself that she was, by no means, the best player on the team. Not a strong shooter, her strength lay in defense and hustle. A powerful rebounder, she dominated under the boards and intimidated the opposing team with her aggressive defense.

But Wendy's strongest asset was determination. She persevered through the challenge.

*Never give up*

You have that tenacity too. When you're working toward a positive goal (such as finishing college), stubbornness can be a good trait. *Stay the Course* on your pathway to complete your degree. You will face challenges and obstacles, but you will meet them and find a way over and through the trials.

You can do it!

I'm praying for you.

> *May God bless your new commitment as a young adult setting course on your college journey. The road is filled with twists and turns, obstacles, and potholes, but with faith, perseverance, and hard work, you will succeed.*

# Acknowledgments

For everyone who has faced the terror of a new journey; perhaps you recall the apprehension you faced as a new high school graduate preparing to further your education. The many college students I've been honored and privileged to serve during my career as a teacher, college professor, and administrator inspire this book. You gifted me with your trust, respect, and commitment to achieving your goals. I am grateful and humbled by the blessing of working with each of you.

For my family, this work would not have been possible without your encouragement and understanding. You've accepted and encouraged me in my calling to serve college students and you understood the long hours dedicated to teaching and mentoring students—from their first immersion into the unknown world of college to their journey across the graduation stage.

To my colleagues at Lenoir-Rhyne University, thank you for the opportunity to teach and serve with you in the College of Health Science. My years with you and the students of LR allowed me to grow in knowledge, faith, and confidence to mentor students. I'm especially grateful to Dr. Jane Jenkins, Dr. Larry Hall, Dr. Gail Summer, and Dr. Michael McGee for your mentorship during my years at Lenoir-Rhyne University.

To Morgan James Publishing, who recognized the need to support and encourage students as they enter college and commit to completing their education—thank you. This is a challenging journey for young adults, and I'm grateful Morgan James is committed to helping students "stay the course" and achieve their goal of graduating. Thank you, Terry Whalin, for your encouragement, enthusiasm, and mentoring. Thank you, David Hancock, for your sincere support of your authors. I am grateful to the entire Morgan James Publishing team for your guidance and assistance.

For my editor, Cortney Donelson, I appreciate your timeliness, encouragement, and expertise. You've helped *Stay the Course* develop into a useful devotional handbook to serve the needs of beginning college students as they progress toward their degrees.

A special and profound thank you to all my teachers, mentors, and colleagues who guided each step of my education and my career. I extend special appreciation to my colleagues at Draper Elementary School and my professors at Appalachian State University and the University of North Carolina at Greensboro. Your dedication, commitment, tenacity, and love enabled me to grow in experience and nurturing skills and put this knowledge and experience to use in serving others.

Finally, for all my students during my forty-four-year teaching career, thank you for your faith and courage and the important life lessons you shared with me. You are the reason I love teaching and mentoring.

# About the Author

D r. Katherine Pasour is a retired college professor, an author, and a speaker. During more than four decades of teaching, greater than half at the college level, Katherine has taught and mentored thousands of students.

Katherine has degrees in health and physical education and religion, and a PhD in education. She has taught health and physical education to children, wellness to young adults, general education courses, and research classes for honors students, and she's prepared students to be teachers.

An outdoor girl at heart, Katherine enjoys her farm animals, gardening, and hiking. Although pulling weeds or spreading mulch in her flowers aren't her favorite hobbies, she finds these outdoor tasks are great stress relievers, especially in the spring when the fruits of her labor display their glorious blossoms.

May God bless you on this new adventure. Please feel free to contact Dr. Pasour by email or join her on social media.

Email: katherinepasour@gmail.com

Website: https://katherinepasour.com/

Facebook AuthorPage: Sheltered By An Angel's Wings, Katherine Pasour Author

Twitter: @katherinepasour

Instagram: KatherinePasourAuthor

# A free ebook edition is available with the purchase of this book.

**To claim your free ebook edition:**

1. Visit MorganJamesBOGO.com
2. Sign your name CLEARLY in the space
3. Complete the form and submit a photo of the entire copyright page
4. You or your friend can download the ebook to your preferred device

  Morgan James BOGO™

A **FREE** ebook edition is available for you or a friend with the purchase of this print book.

CLEARLY SIGN YOUR NAME ABOVE

**Instructions to claim your free ebook edition:**
1. Visit MorganJamesBOGO.com
2. Sign your name CLEARLY in the space above
3. Complete the form and submit a photo of this entire page
4. You or your friend can download the ebook to your preferred device

## Print & Digital Together Forever.

| Snap a photo | Free ebook | Read anywhere |
|---|---|---|